ON THE
CANCER FRONTIER

ON THE
CANCER FRONTIER

ONE MAN, ONE DISEASE, AND A MEDICAL REVOLUTION

PAUL A. MARKS, MD
AND
JAMES STERNGOLD

PUBLICAFFAIRS
NEW YORK

PublicAffairs books are available at special discounts for bulk
purchases in the U.S. by corporations, institutions, and other
organizations. For more information, please contact the Special
Markets Department at the Perseus Books Group, 2300 Chestnut
Street, Suite 200, Philadelphia, PA 19103, call (800) 810-4145,
ext. 5000, or e-mail special.markets@perseusbooks.com.

Book Design by Linda Mark

Library of Congress Cataloging-in-Publication Data

Marks, Paul A., author.
  On the cancer frontier : one man, one disease, and
a medical revolution / Paul Marks and James Sterngold. —
First edition.
    p. ; cm.
Includes bibliographical references and index.
ISBN 978-1-61039-252-5 (hardcover)—
ISBN 978-1-61039-253-2 (e-book)
  I. Sterngold, James, author. II. Title. [DNLM: 1. Marks, Paul A.
2. Neoplasms—history. 3. Antineoplastic Agents—history.
4. Biomedical Research. 5. Cell Transformation, Neoplastic.
6. Medical Oncology—history. 7. Neoplasms--therapy. QZ 11.1]
  RS431.A64
  616.99'4061—dc23
                                                         2013042849

First Edition

10 9 8 7 6 5 4 3 2 1

To my indispensable partner, Joan H. Marks

CONTENTS

Contents

PREFACE

READING ABOUT CANCER in the media can be jarring. One of mankind's oldest known and most deadly diseases is not only discussed far more frequently, it seems, than other serious illnesses (heart disease, for instance); it is often described as though it were part of a moral parable rather than just an enormously challenging medical science problem. The issue is often framed not in terms of the success or failure of a new treatment, or the promise of some new avenue for research, but as a contest between good and evil, competence against incompetence, good intentions versus bad.

Time, for instance, recently blared on its cover, "How to Cure Cancer," with a subhead declaring, "Yes, it's now possible—thanks to new cancer dream teams that are delivering better results faster." Potential magic bullets appeared to have been found by tapping into that great American resource, teamwork, with inspiration coming from some innovative, selfless philanthropists. But only weeks later a sour article in the *New York Times Sunday Magazine* headlined "Our Feel-Good War on Breast Cancer" asked, with a bitter edge, "Has raising awareness become more important than saving lives?" Selflessness and courage were nowhere to be found. A blogger, responding to the article, commented afterward that "there's an epidemic of overtreatment," as though it were a known fact that the problem with cancer care was that some ill-intentioned doctors were doing too much for their patients, not too little.

And it is not just doctors who get judged by such moral standards. When patients overcome cancers, it is often attributed to their strong moral fiber, not good fortune that they had a form of the disease susceptible to current therapies or that they quickly obtained treatment at a good hospital. Some cancer self-help books focus on the curative powers of positive thinking, with an implication that succumbing means the patient failed, not that the disease is vicious and unimaginably difficult to stop. Cancer has fallen into a category with issues like immigration and gun control—everyone is expected to have an opinion.

The media coverage reflects the seemingly random intensity and unpredictability of the disease and a widely shared frustration that American ingenuity has failed to find the final "cure" President Nixon promised when he launched the "war on cancer" nearly a half century ago. The other war at that time, in Vietnam, was mired in an insurgency. The enemy was relentless, absorbing our bombs and then regrouping and fighting back. The war on cancer, everyone expected, would be different. I think many people felt, instinctively, that it would restore our moral edge.

From the start, the campaign against cancer was laced with a sense of heroism by being compared to the race to the moon—a race that, of course, we won. It was to be a medical Manhattan Project, another heroic success. And that has been the problem. If American scientists could build an atomic bomb in just a few years in the New Mexico desert, if they could fly a man into the heavens and land him on the moon ahead of the Soviets, if we could cure smallpox and polio, then surely nothing could prevent us from defeating cancer. How could any barrier stand in the way of American spirit, American technology, and American money?

It was a seductive narrative, which in no way prepared people for the reality that all cancers would never be curable by a single pill. The metaphorical failure of the metaphorical war on cancer felt to many people like a reaffirmation of the rottenness of the end of the Nixon era, as though it were a moral failing on the part of government that denied us a cure. It is story without foundation, one that pays no attention to the singular power and elusiveness of the disease itself.

The truth, uncomfortable and inconvenient as it may be, is that medical science has never faced a more inscrutable, more mutable, or more ruthless adversary. It is a unique disease. Cancer is, in a way, the body's war on itself. The microscopic cellular resources we as a species rely on to multiply, survive, and defeat diseases are more or less shared in equal measure by cancers; cancers—the many maladies lumped together under that name—use all of the cell's capabilities to defeat the treatments we throw at the disease. That has been the medical challenge, to drill deeply into those capabilities and cellular mechanisms, to understand them and then manipulate them. The real secret to cancer's tenacity, and to the therapies that ultimately tame it, lies in our advancing ability to understand its biology. That, in part, is the subject of this book.

But the history of cancer research and treatment, particularly since Watson and Crick's brilliant discoveries about DNA in the 1950s, has not been a straight line leading to an inevitable success. A new drug vanquishes all tumors in laboratory mice, then fails in human trials. A seemingly innocuous and long-overlooked chemical suddenly opens a promising door to a new treatment that produces measurable improvements, but often for rare cancers that affect few people. Some breakthroughs, often developed over a period of years at great expense, extend the lives of patients by just a few months. Particularly maddening are the drug trials that seem to fail—except for a near-miraculous cure of one cancer patient, which can be neither replicated nor explained.

Successes and failures in cancer research are rarely absolute because of the vexing mutability of cancer cells, one of their most fundamental characteristics. Tumors go into remission only to come roaring back later in a changed, more potent form that chemotherapeutic drugs or radiation cannot stop.

That gets at the essence of the medical difficulties: first, there is not one genetic change that causes cancer, but hundreds if not thousands, and second, though cancers can and usually do mutate within each patient, the drugs or other treatments we use against them cannot. Thus, new treatments that hit new targets must be endlessly formulated. Scientists struggle not just to understand and outwit this resourceful disease but, on a more human level, to maintain a positive outlook in the face of constant setbacks.

These are life-and-death issues, and so the cancer campaign does have moral as well as medical dimensions, but the hurdles to progress come largely from the inherently complex nature of cancer. There have been a growing number of improvements in cancer care—and outcomes. They have relied primarily on the extraordinary progress that has been made in understanding the biology of cancer. We take for granted the revolution in our understanding of how tumors develop and grow, but the leaps in our understanding of the inner nature of cells, and their malicious mutations, cancer cells, are one of the greatest achievements in the history of science. They have taken place within just the past few decades.

Scientists have now solved, for the most part, what had been the most enduring and deadly medical mystery of the preceding two thousand years: What is cancer? When you understand that achievement and the vast distance scientists have traveled, you can appreciate how close medical science has come not to "curing" all the many diseases we refer to as cancer, but to reducing and controlling cancers. We stand on the threshold of the age of cancer containment. Cancer patients will live longer, fuller lives. This book explains how.

one

CRACKING MEDICINE'S OLDEST MYSTERY

F ROM MY INITIAL EXAMINATION of the bubbly, whip-smart teenager, I knew her problem was serious. I was in my third year at the College of Physicians and Surgeons, Columbia University's medical school, confident, perhaps even a little arrogant, as I worked my way to the top of my class. It was 1948, and, like most of my classmates, I dreamed of the great things I would accomplish in my white lab coat. As I rotated through the pediatric portion of my clinical training at Columbia-Presbyterian Hospital, I had gotten in the habit of attacking each new case with energy, certain that I could offer some fresh insights to heal the children who entered the ward. But this case was different.

I read the young woman's initial diagnosis and noticed the conspicuously swollen lymph nodes in her neck, her fever, the cough, and, most worrying, the telltale wheezing sound. There was no doubt. It was cancer, a lymphoma. For all my ambition and my freshly developed skills, I knew what this meant: this upbeat young woman was facing a death sentence. Not only did medicine have virtually nothing to offer her, we had no real understanding of where her cancer came from, why it struck, or how it killed. Worst of all, we knew almost nothing about how to slow or stop it.

That vacuum of information regarding a disease that afflicted more than a million people every year in the United States alone was startling. But at the time human cells, and cancer cells in particular, were black boxes of mystery—distant, seemingly impenetrable, and foreboding. As biologist and Nobel laureate Albert Claude later noted, "The cell was as distant from us as the stars and galaxies." We knew more about the structure of the atom than we did about the most fundamental mechanisms of life. There had been no equivalent of an Albert Einstein, Niels Bohr, or J. Robert Oppenheimer yet in the world of cancer.

The clinical protocols dictated that we begin treating my teenage patient with a round of chemotherapy. One of the drugs was derived from a nitrogen mustard gas that, believe it or not, had been developed for warfare. At the time there were no clinical trials or pioneering new treatments we could try. As her physicians, we seemed to be going through the motions of what I was certain would be a futile exercise, and I experienced something unfamiliar: I felt defeated by her cancer. The remarkable thing was, she was not. She was a moonbeam of optimism, confidently promising me during our conversations that she would beat her cancer and furthermore that, once healthy, she was going to study to become a doctor herself.

She was fascinated, she said, by the fact that the "crab" was the Latin symbol of her illness. That was good news, she insisted. The crab crawled slowly, and she, young and fleet, would surely overcome the lymphoma. Each day when I asked her how she was feeling, seeing for myself the toll the disease and the treatments were taking on her frail body, she always found something positive to say. I knew the truth and was struck by the role reversal in our relationship: she spoke with confidence and a touch of bravado, while I was the one struggling to come to grips with the brutal progress of the disease. No medical school classroom had prepared me for these emotions.

Within weeks of the start of her treatment, the chemotherapy had left her with nausea, diarrhea, and bone marrow damage. She was deteriorating by the day. Her white blood cell count was so depleted that had she left the isolation unit of the hospital, she would have been vulnerable to devastating infections. Nevertheless, her parents sought me out one day and asked, really pleaded, if they could take her home for just a few days. It was very important to them. Their daughter's fourteenth birthday was approaching, and they wanted her to celebrate it with family and friends, certain it would cheer her up.

It was a terrible moment. I had no choice but to pass along the judgment of her attending physician, that heading home was not an option. They burst into tears, knowing full well what that implied. I was jolted, too. The message, I felt, was that we were inadequate to the trust that this gravely ill young woman and her family had placed in us because cancer was such an efficient, relentless foe. It was killing with impunity, turning my colleagues and me into bystanders.

After I finished my three months of pediatrics, the courageous young woman was officially no longer my patient, but I made a point of visiting her most days in her hospital room. Often I spoke with her father—a Princeton professor—and we grew close. Day after day, I observed as the cancer did its terrible work. Next to the bed would be her parents and, most difficult of all, her sister, an identical twin. What a painful contrast—in the bed a desperately ill young woman, weakened and withering from a disease that medicine had no answer for, and next to her a healthy mirror image, vigorous and heartbroken. It did not last long. One day, my young cancer patient just seemed to fall asleep as she slipped into a coma and then passed away. I asked myself, was this really the best my profession had to offer?

Medicine has scaled entire ranges of mountains in the past century as it has developed the means to combat an array of injuries and illnesses. We take the progress for granted, but it is a marvel, particularly compared to the previous centuries, during which shamans, charlatans, and ersatz healers battled disease with little to show for the efforts beyond modest incremental improvements in care. We have all but eliminated terrible infectious diseases like smallpox and polio. We have made great progress in understanding and controlling the deadly AIDS epidemic. We tinker with and mend the human body and its organs today like mechanics. Surgeons can take the heart apart and reassemble it with new parts, or replace it altogether. Serious burns were once painful and certain killers, but the survival rate has risen significantly. We crack genetic codes every day. The miraculous, in short, has become routine.

Cancer, however, is in a class by itself. Back in the 1940s, its assaults were so unyielding, so unsparing, that the disease was considered too dark a subject for most people to discuss—even doctors. The idea of a cancer survivor was almost an oxymoron. I never discussed the death of my young lymphoma patient with anyone, but the experience was critical in shaping my career. It persuaded me that I did not have the stomach to deal day to day with cancer sufferers at the clinical level, one at a time, particularly children. The drama behind losing patients never ceased to overpower me, even much later in my career. I recall the pain when a cousin of mine, a doctor in Colorado, a neonatal surgeon, in fact, contacted me at Memorial Sloan-Kettering Cancer Center for treatment of a melanoma.

He had initially just found a spot on his back. When he arrived in New York, we learned that it had already metastasized all over his body, reaching his lymph nodes and his brain. I was in the room with him when he was told of the extent of the disease. He was a middle-aged man with a family, and it was terrible news to have to absorb. He was sitting up in bed, and he looked at me, imploringly, and sputtered, "I don't want to die. I'm too young to die." He passed away the next day. I had built up substantial emotional armor by that time, but his words pierced it. Cancers are brutal emotional opponents as well as daunting physical challenges.

Maybe it was a weakness, but I had to acknowledge my limits. I feared as far back as my student days that my emotional reactions would impair my ability to analyze situations objectively and provide the best treatment options. If I were to have any impact in defeating this illness, it would have to be in the research laboratory and the classroom. I knew that, under any circumstances, the odds would be long. During my student years, to even utter the word *cancer* meant you had crossed a line, going from "This is a difficult medical problem" to "There's not much we can do."

Choosing to pursue cancer research or treatment in the late 1940s was regarded as an eccentric if not unfortunate career detour, particularly for a student with a lot of promise. For decades, the only effective treatment for most cancers was surgical removal of solid tumors, and the track record was limited at best. "Cures" could be achieved only in patients where tumors were discovered so early that they could be removed before any cancer cells had metastasized—which was the case less than 20 percent of the time.

The whole specialty of oncology was regarded with a bit of disdain because the causes of cancer were so mercurial and treatments so limited. If you were smart and gifted, you went into top-drawer specialties like cardiology, surgery, or internal medicine, as almost all of my medical school classmates had done. Focusing solely on curing cancer at that time was akin to a biologist deciding to build a career around the study of "Bigfoot."

Dr. C. P. Rhoads, the first director of the Sloan-Kettering Institute, frankly acknowledged the condescending view some had of his field. "It is seen as the activity of the enthusiast," Rhoads commented in the institution's 1949 annual report. "To engage in it at all is seen as audacious; to enter upon it seriously is seen as Quixotic; to adopt it as a career is deemed fool hardy. The statement is often made that to seek a better knowledge of the control and cure of cancer is as absurd as to search for the spring of eternal youth, or the mystical basis of life itself."

Rhoads was, in a sense, prescient. The search for the origins of cancer—and, thus, the search for vulnerabilities that doctors could then exploit to defeat it—has required that we dive as deeply into the molecular basis of life as science can take us. It calls for research into some of the most profound and fundamental processes of life—the study of how cells replicate, how genes express their functions, what regulates genetic behavior, how cells protect themselves, and how seemingly random "mistakes" in gene replication can cause the transformation of normal cells into lethal cancerous cells.

Seeking the causes of cancer was not unlike physicists deconstructing the atom to understand the fundamental nature of matter, except that the laws of physics are immutable; cancer is a moving target. Cancer cells grow and change constantly, and their mutability is often the key to the deadliness of their attacks. Cancer is, in short, the existential illness. As long as cell division is the means by which we propagate and survive as a species, cancers will develop.

By 1949 we had discovered a great deal about the architecture of the atom and how to unleash its power, but we understood little about the inner activities of the cell, or of DNA. By my last year of medical school, cancer had barely been covered in our curriculum. That year I chaired a group of students presenting the annual honors research seminar. Wanting to focus on the most challenging subject we could think of, we chose cancer.

We organized a series of papers with titles like "Heredity and Neoplasia," "Hormonal Aspects of Neoplasia," and "Viruses as Etiological Agents of Cancer." We pored over medical journals, consulted our professors to refine our understanding, and laid out what were the state-of-the-art theories of the disease.

We were proud of our comprehensiveness, but, in hindsight, the explanations we provided were relatively primitive. Most, in fact, were just plain wrong. We—like many others in the medical profession—even failed to recognize some contemporary discoveries on the makeup of genes that, over time, would open a window into the ways cancers develop and spread.

For instance, in 1943 Oswald Avery and two associates at the Rockefeller Institute (now Rockefeller University) demonstrated that the chemical known as DNA contained the hereditary elements in cells. And it was known as far back as the 1920s that these chemicals resided in the nucleus of the cell. Nevertheless, the scientific field had not embraced those findings. The ideas were new, and there was no scientific consensus. Medical researchers understood that genetic mutations were in some way associated with cancer, but many believed that the components of heredity were located in the cell's cytoplasm, the larger gel-like region surrounding the nucleus. One respected journal that we cited in our honors seminar reported that "the gene is invisible and is recognized by its effects."

We also failed to note, like the authors of the articles we were citing, the new discovery, in 1949, that parts of genes can be reshuffled, or "transposed," essentially creating new genes from the bits and pieces of older ones, with new characteristics. Dr. Barbara McClintock, who would later win a Nobel Prize for her work, discovered these "jumping genes," as some called them, while studying the mutability in the colors of corn kernels. This important insight led to the critical understanding that DNA, the complex of acids and sugars that make up our genes, is not a static structure, as many had supposed. No mention was made of this in our seminar.

As I reread our senior symposium papers today, I am struck by how little we questioned the accepted explanations for cancer. The simple truth was that scientists did not fully understand the differences between healthy cells, which multiply at a methodical pace and are programmed to die after they have served their purposes, and cancer cells, whose signature is a frantic rate of division and a zombielike resistance to the normal death cycle. Nor had the profession yet learned that cancer cells begin as healthy cells before being subverted by genetic mutations.

Our papers were advanced compared to the state of medical thinking in the first decades of the twentieth century. I recently found a small pamphlet published in 1911, *The Facts About Cancer,* which explains that most cancers begin with some sort of irritation of the skin and warns that cancers of the mouth are often initiated by "ragged, dirty teeth," which cause abrasions that can blossom into malignancies. Prevention, it adds, should involve a visit to the dentist and a thorough cleaning.

But my graduating class stood on the cusp of not one but a series of revolutions in our understanding of the cell's biology. The study of cancer was about to enter a new era. A number of major breakthroughs, especially the discovery of the structure of DNA by James Watson and Francis Crick in 1953—the famous double helix—altered the course of cancer research, my career, and, in time, medicine's ability to control cancers. This book will describe those breakthroughs, which

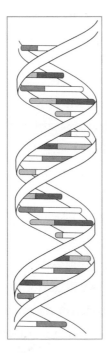

The double helix structure of DNA, the storehouse of human genetic instructions. In healthy cells, DNA replicates millions of times without fault, but in rare instances there are "mistakes," creating mutations that can lead to cancers.

are still unfolding, and explain how a string of brilliant scientific insights has been slowly but progressively translated into treatments that are transforming patients' lives.

From those early days in my career more than sixty years ago, I have witnessed and participated in one of the greatest sustained scientific assaults in history, perhaps misleadingly called the "war on cancer." As dean of Columbia's medical school, vice president of health sciences at the university, director of Columbia's Cancer Center, and then, for twenty years, president of the exceptional Memorial Sloan-Kettering Cancer Center, I helped guide many of these scientific and medical leaps, while contributing a pioneering anticancer drug, known as a "targeted therapy."

"War" is a metaphor that suggests a campaign with a beginning and an end, and it is not uncommon to hear questions about whether the "war on cancer" has really accomplished much; after all, despite an investment of billions of dollars and decades of work, there is still no "cure" for most cancers, no therapy that can prevent them with certainty. It took less than a decade to get to the moon, yet we are more than forty years into this war without a conclusion, or even a clear sign of when it will end, if at all.

That may be true, but it is also, I believe, a misguided way of looking at the issue. Given the malleability of the disease, and its roots in the way cells divide and grow, that is the wrong question. The prospect of finding a single "cure" for all cancers is unlikely. The enemy will always

12

have more faces than we have weapons at any one time. Wars are won and lost; this is a contest with our inner nature, our inner mechanisms. We can, in time, control them, but not "defeat" them.

This is partly a reflection of the fact that, as we have learned, there is no such single thing as "cancer." We commonly talk about "breast cancer" or "colon cancer," but we are finding that no two cancers, even the same clinical types, are exactly the same. At the basic level of their genetic signatures and the proteins they use to conduct their cells' business, we have found that each tumor usually contains many abnormalities, and no two cancers probably match exactly. Studies of many colon and breast cancer tumors have found hundreds of different gene mutations. Just in the ones we have classified so far, it is estimated that there are more than 150 types of cancer.

Adding to this maddening complexity, researchers have found that 99.9 percent of the DNA in cancerous tissue may be identical to the DNA in the normal surrounding cells. That 0.1 percent difference may contain the information that kills, but which altered genes should the researcher or physician target in the patient? Recent research has found that the typical cancer cell has, on average, forty-five abnormalities in the genes and cell pathways that can drive the unrestrained growth of the tumor.

There is, however, cause for optimism, more, in fact, than is commonly understood and a lot more than we had

13

even a decade ago. In terms of important scientific advances, the war has surpassed the expectations that doctors and scientists, my mentors, friends, and colleagues, had in the 1940s or even the 1970s. And that science is, over time, being translated into successful therapies.

The type of childhood lymphoma that struck my young patient when I was a medical student is now a manageable illness with survival rates of 80 percent and more. Young lymphoma patients generally receive a cocktail of drugs to attack their cancers, which are far less toxic than the ones used on my patient. Radiotherapy, which can be sharply focused to suppress or destroy tumors, is often part of the treatment. Scientists at Memorial Sloan-Kettering developed a drug that significantly improves production of white blood cells damaged by chemotherapy treatments—reducing the chances of serious infections. This drug, called G-CSF, or granulocyte colony-stimulating factor, earns the institution about $100 million a year in licensing fees, which supports more research.

Today, if the parents of my young patient were to ask if they could take her home for her birthday, the answer would most likely be simple approval. But it is unlikely that the question would even come up because most childhood lymphomas like hers are treated on an outpatient basis. This young woman would be living at home, giggling over secrets with her fourteen-year-old twin sister and friends.

We know that some cancers are caused by behavior—the most common example is cigarette smoking, estimated to be a causative factor in about 30 to 40 percent of all cancers. Smoking is a pernicious killer that can end lives in a range of ways, often by causing diseases that are long and painful. Obesity and environmental hazards, such as asbestos fibers or carcinogenic chemicals, are also known risk factors. And viruses are causative factors in about 20 percent of human cancers. Human papillomavirus, or HPV infections, is a primary cause of cervical cancer. Hepatitis B or C viruses increase the risk of primary liver cancer. Steps have been taken to reduce exposure to these cancer-causing "insults." But because malignant growths can also begin with the healthy process of cell division and genetic mutations, they will never be entirely eliminated.

In addition, cancer rates rise with age. In fact, aging may be one of the strongest risk factors, so as life expectancies go up, so does the number of cancer cases. About 40 percent of Americans born today will be diagnosed with cancer at some time during their lives, according to the National Cancer Institute (NCI). The more remarkable statistic, though, is the increase in survival rates. The five-year survival rate from all cancers has risen from 35 percent in 1950–1954 to 70 percent in 2002–2008, according to data from the National Cancer Institute. As a result, cancer victims are dying at later ages, and for a growing number of patients, cancer has become a manageable, chronic illness and not a death sentence.

The survival rates for a number of specific cancer types have increased even faster. The five-year survival rate for victims of childhood cancers has climbed from 20 percent to 85 percent. Leukemia survival rates have leaped from 10 percent to 60 percent and from 40 percent to nearly 100 percent for localized prostate cancer. Women with breast cancer have a survival rate of more than 90 percent today, up from 60 percent in the 1950s. The survival rate for those with multiple myeloma has jumped from 5 percent to 45 percent during that time.

The drop in the number of young people dying of cancer is one of the most striking successes. The death rate from cancer for those ages thirty-five to forty-four plummeted by 53 percent from 1950 to 2009. For children five to fourteen, the rate declined by 67 percent. There was an increase for people over eighty-five years old—often because they have been surviving far longer with treatable cancers and succumbing in old age.

Our growing ability to peer deep into cellular behavior at the molecular level has opened the door to even more promising approaches to cancer treatment in the future. First, we are developing a capability to identify the existence of tiny numbers of cancer cells in the blood. That may allow doctors to attack malignancies at an early stage when they are most localized, the least dangerous, and the most vulnerable to therapies. Second, we are moving toward personalized treatments, which begin with genetic and molecular assessments of individual cancers. That allows doctors to determine with some precision which therapies will be most effective. This will increase survival rates in many cases and reduce the amount of time potentially wasted on treatments that miss the targets.

The key to these successes has been breakthroughs in basic science rather than a single-minded focus on producing a "cure." That may sound like a simple distinction, but it has been at the heart of a long battle within the medical community and between researchers and lawmakers in Washington. Often, biologists have pursued research, making remarkable discoveries about obscure enzymes or gene sequencing without knowing how the findings might open doors to new treatments. The applications came later or, frankly, sometimes not at all. That frustrates those who believe that finding cures is the only appropriate task of cancer research and the rest a distraction. The truth is that basic research has been the engine for most of the successes in the war on cancer.

But the clever deceptions of cancer can overcome even the best science. Developing anticancer drugs is not like shooting at a fixed target; it is more like dealing with an insurgency that constantly learns from its losses and adapts to any new defensive strategy. It is a battle against a foe that is just as smart as we are, having all of our coded genetic capabilities and advantages. Consider the successful drug Herceptin, which has proven highly effective against some breast cancers. For years we were not sure why it worked only in some cases. Researchers finally discovered that the drug blocked a specific cellular signaling mechanism, or "receptor," that stimulated breast cancer cell growth, but only about 35 percent of women with breast cancer have that particular "receptor." We can now test patients to see whether they have the receptor and will therefore respond to the drug. Meanwhile, researchers are working to identify the vulnerabilities in the 65 percent of patients whose breast cancer does not have that factor.

Contrary to the narratives one may hear about misguided research or dead ends, the steady translation of scientific insights into therapies is the reason we are unequivocally winning the campaign against cancer. When President Nixon signed the National Cancer Act of 1971, providing for increased research funding, he and others talked excitedly about the equivalent of a "moon shot" effort to find a cure. Appealing and hopeful as that sounded, it was unrealistic at that time because we simply did not understand enough about the cell, our genes, or the causes of the "mistakes" in cell division that transform healthy cells into malignant ones.

The past four decades have dramatically changed the situation. It has been a "war" in which, unlike some other government programs, the money has been well spent, corruption insignificant, and the long-term benefits proven; it is one of the most successful federally funded initiatives ever undertaken, a success represented by the roughly 12 million cancer survivors in the country, compared with about 3 million in 1971, according to the National Cancer Institute.

Over the past several decades, we have made dozens of "moon shot"–caliber discoveries that combined insightful basic science with skillful laboratory development of diagnostic and treatment tools. We have also learned that the best treatments do not only come in pill bottles. During my two decades as president of Memorial Sloan-Kettering, we developed novel methods for treating not just the disease, but also the whole patient.

In order to make this subtle but important shift in our thinking, we had to recognize that outcomes improved when patients were physically and emotionally bolstered to fight their cancers alongside the clinicians. We have witnessed what an enormous difference it makes when patients are willing to take on this fight and are physically able to endure the often highly toxic medications and possible relapses, as well as any new treatment regimens if cancers come back.

Memorial Sloan-Kettering pioneered what are called disease-management teams, in which different specialists work jointly to care for a patient. These teams provide for much better communication among the diagnosticians and oncologists who are focused on a patient's particular cancer. We developed the first cancer pain-management program, the first freestanding breast cancer center, the first adult out-patient clinics for administering chemotherapy, and a psychiatric program for helping patients, relatives, and friends manage the shock and depression that can be produced by a cancer diagnosis. These programs contributed to increases in survivorship rates and have been adopted by cancer centers across the country.

Things might have turned out differently when President Nixon first declared his war. I was dean of Columbia's medical school at that time and, frankly, was concerned that the country was expecting a "cure" in short order. I knew that was all but impossible. I also worried that the newly available federal funding would distort the priorities of research-based academic institutions, such as Columbia. Science might be abandoned in favor of frantic trial-and-error efforts to find "the cure." I wrote a letter to the chairman of the president's Cancer Panel in Washington, DC, charged with overseeing the implementation of the "war" on cancer, expressing my concerns and offering some proposals for avoiding this trap. It was an impulsive gesture rather than a result of any clearly thought-out strategy, but that letter altered my career and, perhaps, helped influence the direction the "war" would take.

two

DECIPHERING THE INNER WORKINGS OF THE CELL

I N THE FIRST HALF OF THE twentieth century, trial and error and some good observations had produced a few insights, but only modest improvements in the treatment of cancer. There were theories that the disease had genetic roots, but there was little detailed proof or mechanistic explanations of just how a defective gene could cause a complex disease like cancer. Scientists had few if any tools to test or improve upon those theories or to turn them into therapies. But the discovery of DNA's double-helix structure by Watson and Crick in 1953 unleashed new research into how genes express themselves and accomplish the tasks for which they are programmed.

Researchers began unlocking the complex chemistry of DNA, the architecture of DNA molecules, and learning how our heredity, our genes, create perfect copies and communicate tasks within cells. This molecular biology revolution placed genetics, the study of enzymes, and the regulation of cellular behavior at the heart of our evolving understanding of normal cells.

By the 1950s and 1960s, scientists, for the first time in human history, were able to provide penetrating answers to the question, "How do cells do what they do?" These discoveries, in turn, made it possible for researchers to identify the abnormalities in cancer cells—among the first solid steps in ending the terror of cancer and the futility in treating it. With this understanding, we were no longer making wild stabs at the essence of cancer. It is when the real history of the campaign against cancer begins.

These discoveries swept me up just as I began my research career in 1953. I had joined an officer training program as an undergraduate during World War II, like many of my peers, and the government paid for my medical education at Columbia. In return, I was required to perform military service as a doctor after graduating. It was 1952 and the Korean War was raging, but I was assigned to the National Institutes of Health in Washington as an officer in the US Public Health Service, then a branch of the military.

The NIH may seem to many like a faceless bureaucratic entity in the federal government's vast research complex, but it is one of the most successful scientific institutions in history, and in the 1950s and 1960s it was filled with the leaders in biomedical research. For aspiring scientists seeking the most sophisticated training, it was *the* place to be.

There was a sense that we were opening frontiers in understanding and treating a range of diseases in new, more effective ways. Lewis Thomas, the physician-scientist and essayist, wrote of the NIH, "All by itself, this magnificent institution stands as the most brilliant social invention of the 20th century anywhere."

I had the further good fortune to work under a key figure in the new era of biological discoveries, Arthur Kornberg, whose lab was focusing on the enzymes involved in the replication of DNA. Enzymes are specialized proteins that act as catalysts for the chemical processes in the human body, from creating new DNA to converting food into energy. Without thousands of enzymes, our biological reactions would happen too slowly to support life. Their functions are very specific and intricate, even minor, but the malfunction of any one of our enzymes can be fatal.

Among researchers, the 1950s are sometimes referred to as the time of the "enzyme hunters," because we were accelerating our understanding of the importance and identities of the chemical pathways, and the reactions that take place within them, that make cells function. In 1959 Kornberg received a Nobel Prize for his discovery of the enzymes that help form the chemical building blocks of DNA. His findings laid the groundwork for advances in molecular biology and biotechnology.

Soon after I joined his laboratory, Kornberg left the NIH for Washington University in St. Louis, but he was replaced by Bernard Horecker, an outstanding biochemist. By studying cells in a simpler organism, in this case, spinach leaves, we discovered three new sugars and three new enzymes in a metabolism pathway called the pentose phosphate pathway, through which cells burn sugars. In the first step along the spinach-cell pentose phosphate pathway, an enzyme called G6PD, we discovered, was the catalyst.

I returned to Columbia in 1955 and began my own independent research career as a junior faculty member. I decided to try to determine if human cells had the same chemical pathway as spinach leaves and used the enzyme G6PD. I chose to look at human red blood cells. It was a pragmatic choice, as I could draw blood from my willing colleagues or use leftover blood samples that had been sent to the hospital's laboratory for diagnostic purposes.

As I began my search, I made two interesting discoveries: one, I found G6PD in human red blood cells, suggesting that the spinach leaves and human blood used the same pathway, and two, some of the blood donors were deficient in the enzyme.

One of these donors was, as it happened, my laboratory technician. Further testing showed that her son had a G6PD deficiency, too. I also found that blood from several members of a Greek family we tested had low G6PD levels, which produced what I determined was a type of anemia. Our findings strongly suggested that this medical condition was hereditary. Testing three generations of the Greek family, the pattern of the G6PD deficiency indicated that the inherited trait was passed on from parent to child by a defective gene located on the "X" chromosome, the sex chromosome. (Humans have twenty-two paired chromosomes in the nuclei of our cells and two sex chromosomes, an X and Y chromosome in males and two X chromosomes in females.) This confirmed that the path to the anemia could be traced directly back to an abnormal gene. It was an epiphany for me, as relatively little was known about the genetic causes behind certain diseases.

When I returned to Columbia, I was recruited by Alfred Gellhorn, a professor of medicine, the younger brother of Martha Gellhorn, the well-known war correspondent and the third wife of Ernest Hemingway. He had been given the job of building the staff at a new cancer hospital and research facility, Francis Delafield Hospital at the Columbia-Presbyterian Medical Center.

Delafield, located on Fort Washington Avenue and West 164th Street, was one of two cancer hospitals built by New York City after World War II to provide high-quality cancer care alongside research and training. I joined the medical oncology service, and Gellhorn gave me the job of making chemotherapy part of the teaching and clinical practice at Columbia.

It turned out to be a quixotic pursuit, and I learned hard lessons about why some institutions resisted big commitments to cancer research. Treatment options for cancer patients were still extremely limited. If a malignancy could not be removed with surgery (which was the case about 75 percent of the time), we could offer little more than short-term palliative therapy. The chemotherapeutic agents that were available were generally highly toxic, and even when we could induce remissions, they were usually brief. And, to our dismay, we did not even understand why the drugs worked or why they failed. That led some doctors to develop a deep mistrust of chemotherapy and pessimism about whether it could ever be a cancer-fighting tool. Some leaders of the medical school and the hospital blatantly resisted the effort to expand our cancer treatment and research: neither Presbyterian Hospital nor the clinical departments of the medical school integrated Delafield's research and cancer-patient care into their mainstream medical activities. To make matters worse, some of the surgeons openly resented our efforts to test and introduce new anticancer drugs. They regarded such drugs as ineffective at best, and possibly misleading for the patients, or as poisons that harmed patients unnecessarily, as they often produced painful side effects.

The surgical oncology service at Delafield was headed by Cushman Haagensen, an eminent doctor well known for his commitment to what was known as "radical" surgery for removing breast cancer. In this procedure, which was state-of-the-art treatment at that time, but is rarely if ever performed now, the surgeon removes all the breast tissue along with lymph nodes in the armpit and chest-wall muscles. It not only badly disfigured the patient, but also achieved five-year survival rates of less than 60 percent. (Today, surgery or a lumpectomy, followed by radiotherapy or chemotherapy, can produce a 90 percent or better five-year survival rate for localized breast tumors.) It was hard to break out of this therapeutic rut because of the skepticism of some of the surgeons toward chemotherapy, which, admittedly, did not have an impressive track record. The friction led to a difficult and symbolic personal confrontation. One day, Haagensen found me administering a drug in a clinical trial to a patient with an advanced cancer. Of course, all appropriate approvals had been obtained, including consent from the patient, but Haagensen, in front of the desperate patient, angrily ordered me out of the ward, along with the drug. The trial had to be stopped. This was not going to be easy.

three

THE FIRST LOOK DEEP
INSIDE THE CANCER CELL

A S THE NUMBER OF SIGNIFICANT discoveries in molecular biology and genetics grew in the 1960s, one of the most productive and exciting biomedical research organizations was the Pasteur Institute, housed in a series of modest redbrick buildings on rue du Docteur Roux in the Fifteenth Arrondissement of Paris. It was founded by Louis Pasteur, the great nineteenth-century biologist, who developed a vaccine for rabies, discovered that microorganisms cause many infectious diseases, and described the role of yeast in fermentation. The institute had become a magnet for scientists inspired by the promise of molecular biology. The institute's intellectual leaders, Jacques Monod, François Jacob, and André Lwoff, were addressing, in new and insightful ways, fundamental questions about our cellular factories. We knew critical information was encoded into our DNA, but we did not yet understand how the different parts of the cell spoke to each other and conveyed these instructions or how cellular processes were regulated. How exactly do genes control enzyme synthesis? How does the information encoded in our DNA get translated into the instructions for producing the proteins that conduct the work of cells? The research at the institute also touched on problems like the one I had been trying to solve—how a gene defect caused the deficiency of the enzyme G6PD and anemia. Monod and his colleagues were pulling the veil off these mysteries, and, for me, the questions they were exploring verged on the fantastic.

Armed with a $15,000 fellowship from the Commonwealth Foundation, I took a leave from the medical school, and, in May 1961, my wife and I and our two young children swapped our house in Scarsdale, New York, for a spacious pre–World War I apartment in Neuilly, a suburb of Paris.*

Monod, Jacob, and Lwoff had discovered that the detailed information contained in DNA of bacteria was translated and then transmitted by a specialized molecule whose structure was similar to DNA but differed in three

---

*The apartment belonged to a French postdoctoral fellow, Étienne-Émile Baulieu, who was spending a year at Columbia. He would later win acclaim for championing the "day-after" contraceptive pill, RU486.

ways: first, it substituted ribose, a type of sugar molecule, for deoxyribose; second, one of its four nucleotides—the components of the twisting legs of the ladder in the double helix—was different; and third, it had only a single strand of the ladder rather than two strands, as in DNA's double helix.

They also discovered that this new molecule transported the genetic information contained in DNA from the nucleus of a cell, where the genes are located, to the cytoplasm,

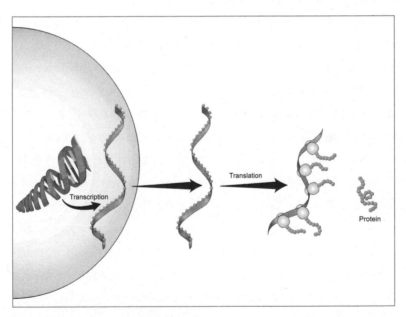

DNA uses messenger RNA to deliver instructions to the cell: Through transcription, DNA "downloads" its messages onto strands of RNA, which then carry the instructions to ribosomes. That is where cells maintain the machinery that produce the proteins that carry out cellular functions.

where proteins are assembled. It was like sending a blue-print from an engineering headquarters to the factory floor for the manufacturing of a product. For this reason, they called their new molecule "messenger" RNA, or mRNA.

This represented a profound new understanding of the biology of healthy cells. We did not know it yet, but this was another in the string of discoveries that began to shed light on the enigma of cancer. Basic science was far ahead of any therapies, but it was essential in leading the way toward effective and less toxic cancer treatments.

Monod's laboratory, on the ground floor of a building across the street from the master's old facilities, was a vibrant intellectual training ground, crowded with talented students and visitors. We held daily group lunches—feasts, actually, with food from a nearby charcuterie—where we crowded together to share ideas and debate our work.

We generally shared the view that by looking at cells from the inside out—scrutinizing the microscopic causes of cancer and other diseases rather than the outwardly visible symptoms—we could achieve previously unimaginable insights into how some diseases caused harm, and thus insights in how they could be cured. This intellectual leap represented a paradigm shift: we believed that we could ultimately identify the basic genetic "mistakes" that caused many diseases, including cancers.

Given my research into the genetic roots of the G6PD enzyme deficiency, and the resulting anemia, Monod suggested that I try to determine if the gene that transmitted the bad information that caused the deficiency used a defective messenger RNA. The more fundamental aim was to see if the genetic transmission process they had found in bacteria also existed in human cells.

The mRNA in bacteria was found to have a very short half-life, a matter of minutes; the genetic information was "translated" to make protein, and then it quickly degraded. We asked, does a similar short-lived mRNA exist in mammalian cells, delivering information to make proteins from the genes to the "factory floor" in the cell's cytoplasm?

We chose to use red blood cells from rabbits for our research. Red blood cells produce predominantly a single type of protein—globin—which is not difficult to measure, and we could raise rabbits easily in the laboratory. It did not take long to find that the rabbit red blood cells did contain mRNA. Fundamentally, the process was the same in bacteria and in mammalian cells: the information contained in the gene flowed, via mRNA, from the nucleus to the cytoplasm, where it directed synthesis of essential proteins. But there was one clear difference: in these mammalian red blood cells, the mRNA molecules survived for several days, far longer than their counterparts in bacteria, and were much more stable. We speculated that the more complex mammalian cells needed a longer-acting messenger because they were delivering far larger bundles of information.

The implications were exhilarating. These findings opened the door to a deeper understanding of how genes communicate their information and what chemical processes control gene expression. In the years ahead, findings such as these would have a profound impact on cancer research, as we developed an understanding of how the mutations in DNA sent out faulty information that transformed normal cells into cancer cells.

These studies could not have been done a decade earlier, when I was at the National Institutes of Health. Both conceptually and technically, biomedical research was advancing to the point where we could start to think about exploring the twisted biology of cancers and, with luck, attack them in new ways.

four

BRINGING THE NEW SCIENCES TO AN OLD SCHOOL

M Y FAMILY AND I BID A RELUCTANT farewell to Paris in 1962, and I returned to Columbia with a new mission, to spread the gospel of molecular biology and continue with my own research into the genetic sources of disease. I wanted to instill in my students that new paradigm for approaching illnesses, which was then at the frontiers of medicine, but the reality of academic life intruded. I was given a new and larger laboratory in the medical school's main building on my return, but when it came to teaching I was assigned the basic course in clinical pathology. The course covered the techniques for performing routine diagnostic tests, such as blood counts and urine analysis.

Certainly, the class gave the students important, if basic, clinical diagnostic tools, but having just taken part in groundbreaking research, I was reluctant to go back to such mundane pursuits. I wanted to share my enthusiasm and teach students about fresh genetic insights, not explain the mechanics of test tubes, pipettes, and drawing blood. If I was going to teach this course, I decided, it was not going to be without my own small touch of rebellion. I introduced into my lectures discussions of the genetics and molecular biology behind human disease and how these sciences opened a window into the roots of many illnesses. My modest insurrection seemed to inspire at least a few students to share my enthusiasm for basic science as a gateway to understanding and controlling diseases. One of my students was Harold Varmus, who would later win a Nobel Prize for his insights into how normal cells are transformed into cancerous zombies and who would also, years after that, succeed me as president of the Memorial Sloan-Kettering Cancer Center. Varmus wrote in a memoir that the clinical pathology course "made a special impression on me" by demonstrating that "changes in DNA (mutations) could cause disease when they affected physiologically important proteins."

Another student, Robert Lefkowitz, would go on to win a Nobel Prize in Chemistry in 2012. In an interview with Columbia's alumni magazine, he cited my course for having helped introduce to him the idea that studying the molecular and chemical basis of life was a useful way to search for the roots of disease and treatments. I was lucky to have had talented students who picked up on my enthusiasm and then made new discoveries of their own.

In the lab, instead of returning to my work on the G6PD enzyme deficiency in red blood cells, I focused on a potentially fatal form of anemia called thalassemia, which is caused by a failure of red blood cells to produce normal amounts of hemoglobin. I wanted to try to find out if this disease was caused by a defect in the mRNA that transmitted the instructions—the genetic blueprint—for globin production. If the answer to that question was yes, it would provide another demonstration of the value of looking for the genetic defect behind an important disease rather than the traditional medical approach of focusing on fixing the symptoms. The research got at one of my core concerns: showing how basic scientific research could drive the process toward understanding serious disorders and leading the way to effective treatments. I discovered that in the red blood cells of patients with thalassemia, the ribosomes— the sites in cells where proteins are produced under instructions from mRNA—did not make normal amounts of globin. That was the heart of the illness. But when I removed these ribosomes and attached them to messenger RNA from healthy red blood cells, they started producing normal amounts of globin. This indicated that thalassemic anemia was the result of a defective gene. That abnormal gene passed along its inaccurate instructions to the messenger RNA, which then provided an incorrect order to the ribosome, resulting in inadequate production of globin. Most patients with thalassemia have mild symptoms or no symptoms and generally require little treatment. Severe forms, however, can be life threatening. Our understanding of the disease's roots in a genetic defect has led to the development of a blood stem-cell transplant technique to replace faulty stem cells with healthy ones. Researchers today are working to find methods to insert a healthy globin gene into stem cells in patients' own bone marrow, which should allow them to make normal amounts of hemoglobin.

Exciting as I found this research, I was disappointed by the environment at Columbia. In contrast to my experience at the Pasteur Institute, where I was surrounded by colleagues eager to discuss the molecular mechanisms of cells, back home not many of my colleagues were pursuing research at the molecular level and the medical school provided essentially no courses in the burgeoning field of human genetics.

I took every opportunity to lobby for the inclusion of genetics courses, from staff planning discussions to private conversations with the dean. I became well known for my interest in the subject and my pressure. Finally, the school agreed to include a new course in genetics; the professor assigned to teach it was a gynecologist. Columbia, of course, was not alone. Many American medical schools, reflecting the inherent conservatism in the medical community, had yet to embrace molecular biology's new scientific paradigm, despite its promise.

The breakthrough that helped spur the school toward the new science came unexpectedly, in 1967. The College of Physicians and Surgeons was preparing to celebrate the two hundredth anniversary of the granting of its first medical degrees. As part of the events marking the occasion, Dean H. Houston Merritt proposed that the school hold a symposium on a cutting-edge medical subject. It would transform Columbia and send ripples through a medical community just starting to grapple with the power of genetics as a key to understanding cancer.

Dean Merritt had appointed a committee of professors to plan the agenda and invite speakers, but as the deadline loomed they had made little progress and the administration was starting to panic. Dean Merritt then turned to me. I had not been on the original planning committee, but he felt that, given my experience at the Pasteur Institute and my admittedly annoying persistence in pressing genetics and molecular biology, perhaps I would have the contacts to assemble a credible group of speakers. I was named chairman of a new committee and promptly began inviting the most important researchers in the new fields. It was a tremendous opportunity, and I welcomed the task, especially given the resistance I had faced since returning from Paris.

The three-day "Symposium on Genetics and Development," which began on October 18, 1967, was a seminal event for Columbia and a historic marker in the still nascent campaign against cancer. In the first tangible sign of its impact, more than two thousand people had registered, and we had to hastily move the location from our alumni auditorium, which had a capacity of about four hundred, to the gigantic armory across the street at Fort Washington Avenue and West 168th Street. Our roster of speakers was a remarkable all-star team, representing the best of the young molecular biology revolution. It was like having Cy Young, Joe DiMaggio, Sandy Koufax, and Willie Mays playing baseball on the same field.

Francis Crick opened the symposium with a discussion of how information flowed from DNA to RNA, leading to the formation of specific proteins. (His famous colleague James Watson was in the audience.) Severo Ochoa, who had shared the Nobel Prize with Arthur Kornberg, gave a presentation on his recent discoveries of the mechanism of RNA synthesis. Jacques Monod, my mentor at the Pasteur Institute, described his Nobel-winning work on how specific small molecules control gene expression. As he summed it up in his comments: "We know fairly well all the ways the cell operates within itself, but very little is known about how cells communicate with one another." How they form living creatures was, he said, one of the great scientific challenges in the years ahead.

The symposium then moved from the molecular to the cellular level. François Jacob, also from the Pasteur Institute, described his new discoveries on the distribution of genetic materials in the cell and control of gene expression, and Sydney Brenner, a future Nobel laureate, explained his theory of how DNA provides the signals needed to build specific proteins. These discussions were important because, as we were starting to understand, cancer kills by thwarting these normal cellular functions.

Georg Klein, from Sweden's Karolinska Institute, described the way cancers evade the immune system and also how medicine might find a way to enlist the natural tools of immunity to control the spread of tumors.

The next symposium topic was the mechanisms by which viruses induce some types of cancerous tumors, then one of the more important areas of cancer research. And my former college roommate and a Nobel laureate Joshua Lederberg, who was teaching at Stanford, discussed the new concept of "genetic engineering." He described how, in theory, scientists might "fix" faulty genetic material in humans by introducing viruses that would inject the correct genes into the DNA of abnormal human cells.

In all, seven Nobel laureates and five future laureates spoke, a remarkable collection of intellectual firepower. We had come a long way since my senior-year honors symposium on cancer in 1949. Most of the research we discussed at that time was simply wrong. We had little understanding

of the structure and role of genes and DNA and how mutations transformed healthy cells into killers. By contrast, most
of the information that was presented at the symposium in
1967 has proved to be durable and conceptually correct. Very
little of it had yet led to effective new cancer therapies—that
would come—but the scientific breakthroughs discussed in
the armory made clear that a campaign against cancer was
possible. We were developing the intellectual artillery to
match the shrewdness of our foe, though it would take us
many years to fully exploit it.

The symposium signified the concentration of talented
scientists focusing on the basic biology of cancer and the
cascade of new insights that would follow on how healthy
cells and malignant cells function. The building blocks for
anticancer treatments were falling into place.

Scientists were breaking through centuries of dead ends
and were plumbing the chemical mechanisms of life in
ways that started to give the medical field new tools, or
at least ideas for tools, to attack cancer. Max Perutz, for instance, a British molecular biologist and refugee from the
Nazis, discovered the actual shape and structure of complex proteins like hemoglobin, which allowed us to understand the fundamental chemical behavior of enzymes and
other specialized cellular actors. Perutz received a Nobel
Prize in 1962.

Peyton Rous, a Nobel laureate in 1966, showed that a
virus could cause a particular type of cancer in chickens.

Marshall Nirenberg won a Nobel Prize in 1968 for his important work in breaking the genetic code and understanding how genes direct the production of specific proteins.

George Palade, Albert Claude, and Christian de Duve provided the tools for peering inside cells and seeing them as finely tuned machines of many distinct parts rather than masses of jelly, which was how they had appeared under microscopes. These three provided what was effectively a functional map of the cell and its many parts and charted the pathways by which these parts communicate with each other, so-called molecular trafficking. These three scientists were awarded a Nobel in 1974.

These achievements in basic science prompted David Baltimore, who himself won a Nobel Prize in 1975 for his research on tumor viruses, to describe the postwar decades, through the 1970s, as "the heroic times in modern biology." As Baltimore put it, "The Big Questions were posed and answered."

The symposium and the recognition it brought Columbia hit the school like a thunderclap, and the next year Dean Merritt won support from the Board of Trustees of the university to establish, at long last, a Department of Human Genetics and Development. I was appointed chairman, just a year after having earned tenure, as a professor of medicine. It was the beginning of my academic leadership.

I had become convinced that medical education ought to include more work in the sciences of genetics and molecular biology because of the windows they were opening into the nature of diseases. But I had no idea how quickly I would have the chance to put that new agenda into practice.

That opening was created in the aftermath of the fiery Vietnam War protests at Columbia, which came to a head in the spring of 1968. In April groups of students took over a cluster of buildings on the main university campus. From our twelfth-floor apartment on Claremont Avenue, my wife and I could see the "revolutionary flags" draped across the facade of the administration building and students sitting on the window ledges of the president's office.

On the night of April 30, 1968, after talks to restore order had failed, Columbia's president, Grayson Kirk, and his administration called in the New York City police. About two in the morning, I received a call from a frightened student, asking if I could come over to witness what he claimed was police brutality. I rushed over with my small black physician's bag and found the police carting away the student activists.

I observed only minor injuries, other than one broken nose, but the real damage went far deeper than cuts and scrapes. The ordeal led to a serious examination of the university's mission and how it was implemented, and many students insisted, over and over, that Kirk, a symbol of a dying order, had to step down. Columbia was hit with another violent student protest just a month later, and again the students demanded that Kirk leave. He finally decided that his presence was disruptive, and in August 1968 he resigned. He hoped, he said, that by leaving it would ensure "the prospect of more normal university operations."

Since Columbia's founding in the eighteenth century, the leaders made key decisions and handed down their instructions. Following Kirk's departure, the faculty retained Archibald Cox, a Harvard Law School professor and the former solicitor general of the United States, to study how Columbia was run, and he issued a critical report the next year. The Cox commission concluded that the administration "too often conveyed an attitude of authoritarianism and invited mistrust." The top-down style of management would have to end, which was what Kirk's successor, Andrew Cordier, started to do, saying he would be more inclusive in making major appointments and decisions.

When Dean Merritt of the medical school surprised everyone by announcing his retirement, at age sixty-eight, the medical faculty elected a committee to search for a successor. This was one of the clear signs that Columbia was changing, as previously such decisions were made by the administration without faculty input or control. I was named chairman of the committee, and we quickly went to work. A year later, after examining 150 very qualified nominees, we offered the Board of Trustees three outstanding candidates for consideration as dean of the faculty of medicine and vice president of medical affairs.

Although we felt we had followed a methodical, rational process that promised consensus, our candidates quickly ran into the buzz saw of Columbia's byzantine internal politics, particularly the dysfunctional relationship between the medical school and its teaching hospital, Presbyterian.

The hospital had its own independent Board of Trustees and its own leadership structure. Technically, the hospital's authority stopped at the doors of the medical school, but things worked differently in practice, as we quickly discovered. The chairman of the hospital board (an important pro bono position among New York City's health care institutions) at the time was the imperious Augustus "Gus" Long, who was chairman of the Texaco oil company. He adamantly objected to all three of the committee's recommendations for dean.

One, Dr. John Knowles, president of the Massachusetts General Hospital, supported universal health insurance, so he was deemed too liberal. Dr. John Hogness, a medical school alumnus and president of the University of Washington in Seattle, wanted to lead the hospital as well as the medical school to provide much-needed coordination of their activities, but that prospect was perceived as a threat to Long's power, so he was rejected. The third nominee, Dr. Howard Hiatt, chairman of medicine at the Beth Israel Hospital, a Harvard teaching hospital, argued for the same consolidation even more forcefully. In an impassioned letter he wrote to me, he explained that to improve the governance of the medical center, "Columbia University and the Presbyterian Hospital . . . should act as a unit and the authority for both should rest with the same individual."

Hiatt further warned that because of the existing division, the reforms that some of my colleagues and I had worked for, such as introducing genetics and more basic science into the curriculum and pushing the development of new drugs and treatments from that research, were in jeopardy, no matter who was named dean. "It seems to me," he wrote, "that if this point is lost, then all that you and your colleagues have done in the past year . . . will have been lost. I am certain it is tempting to you and your colleagues to refrain from rocking the boat further. . . . However, to proceed as though things were now ideally arranged for the new regime would result . . . in the loss of what should be the great opportunity in American medicine." Many people agreed with him.

Another governance problem had bothered me for years: the leadership of the university expressed little interest in the medical school, located fifty-two blocks to the north of the main campus, and took few steps to learn about or engage actively with the faculty and students.

Before 1972, for example, the university's trustees had never met at their own medical school, and many had never even visited the campus at West 168th Street. The school was something of an orphan in spite of the fact that the health sciences faculties represented more than 50 percent of the entire Columbia University budget and a greater percentage of its income.

Long told the medical school and our search committee that he rejected the search committee's candidates. So Andrew Cordier, the university's new president, in an apparent effort to build a consensus for change, named a committee to study the medical center's unwieldy structure. It was chaired by Dr. J. George Harrar, president of the Rockefeller Foundation. In August 1969 the committee issued its rather harsh findings. Its report stated:

> Many persons involved in the Columbia Presbyterian Medical Center . . . feel strongly that it has not maintained and improved its position locally, nationally, and internationally, as could and should have been expected during the past decade or more. They believe that there has been a growing schism between Columbia Physicians and Surgeons and Presbyterian Hospital and that this has, in fact, damaged the institutions. . . . Some feel that the center and especially the College of Physicians and Surgeons has lost ground within the medical education community and has failed to enhance its international luster during its past decade or more.

The report went on to remark, "The atmosphere at the center seems still to be one in which friction, sometimes a sense of hostility, between the university and the hospital, is all too apparent." The committee recommended that a single director be appointed to oversee both the medical school and the hospital.

Gus Long rejected out of hand any merging of the two institutions and, further, made it clear he would obstruct any of the nominating committee's choices as dean of the medical school. We were stuck. Technically, Cordier could have acted on his own, but I think he knew open strife could have been paralyzing and an enormous distraction when he had so many other urgent issues to confront in those tumultuous times. A mutually acceptable choice was preferred. The administration resolved to try to find a candidate both Long and the search committee would approve, or at least could live with. In my absence the search committee met and came up with a plan: they recommended that Cordier invite me to be dean, in part because of my leadership of the two hundredth anniversary symposium.

My initial reaction was ambivalence. Accepting the appointment would limit my time for research just when I felt it was showing considerable promise. I also had doubts about my ability to handle all facets of the job of dean of the medical school. I had little administrative experience and was not sure I had the temperament. On the other hand, the medical school needed strong leadership, and I had a clear agenda.

I felt I might be able to move Columbia to the cutting edge of research. So I struck a compromise: I said I would accept the deanship, but for only a three-year term. With my letter of acceptance, in 1970, I sent a second letter to the newly recruited university president, William McGill, submitting my resignation, dated June 30, 1973. He agreed to the arrangement, and Long appeared to acquiesce. I believe he thought that, relative to other candidates, I might be easier to control.

I became the seventeenth dean of the College of Physicians and Surgeons and the first Jewish head of the school in its 203 years. I quickly went to work, focusing largely on recruiting academic stars for the faculty and diversifying the student body.

We recruited new leadership for the major clinical departments—medicine, surgery, pediatrics, and obstetrics and gynecology. Two of the new professors, Eric Kandel, who conducted fascinating research on the nature of memory, and Richard Axel, who worked on how the brain senses smell, went on to win Nobel Prizes. Sol Spiegelman, an outstanding molecular biologist, became head of the long-dormant Institute of Cancer Research. Robert Krooth, a card-carrying geneticist, succeeded me as chairman of the Department of Human Genetics and Development. We also developed a new curriculum that expanded the emphasis on molecular biology in numerous courses and taught its clinical implications.

Within days of the announcement of my appointment as dean, I received a call from Gus Long's secretary. I was summoned to report to his office that same afternoon. I found Long seated behind a desk at one end of a large room. There were no other chairs, so I asked if I should get one. "No, you will not be here that long," he said.

Long told me that, notwithstanding the fact that his position was at the hospital rather than the medical school, he had the power to block my appointment as dean. Why, I asked, would he want to do that? The process to find a dean had already been long and disruptive. He said, to my amazement, that he would not allow Columbia to become like NYU, which he pronounced "N-Y-Jew," referring to New York University's medical school.

Stunned, I replied, "Mr. Long, the dean at NYU Medical School is not Jewish." It was Lewis Thomas, the eminent biologist and essayist. I was not sure what else to say, so I tried not to flinch visibly in response to this ugly slight—a clear attempt, I believed, to bully me.

Long had gotten what he wanted, letting me know what I was up against. He responded, "Well, Marks, you have balls," and he left it at that.

Long's attitude was a vestige of a previous era. I had encountered signs of it more than twenty years earlier, when I entered the medical school. My class of 109 included 19 women. Although the medical school had admitted women since 1917, there were rarely more than 2 or 3 in a class. Years later, when I became dean, I discovered the explanation for our class's bounty of females. In the school's

51

archives, I found a letter written in 1945 by the then dean of admissions, Charles Flood, to Willard Rappleye, the dean of the faculty, recommending that the medical school accept more women, because "otherwise the military will send us many minority students."

Long's chairmanship of the hospital board came to a sudden close a couple of years later. I had been asked to attend a meeting of the board. When Long entered the room, the other directors already in place, he asked about two of the board members who were not in the room yet, Vernon Jordan, who is black, and Henry Kissinger, who is Jewish, using crude slurs.

The reaction from the room was shocked silence. After a pause, Mrs. Byron Stookey, the widow of a great neurosurgeon and a trustee for many years, stood up behind her chair. She was a tall, elegant woman, and in a soft but clearly agitated voice, she said, "My father was one of the founders of Babies Hospital, which is part of this hospital. I know he would not tolerate such bigotry." She then added, "I am making a motion that Mr. Long be asked to resign." Harold Helm, the former chairman of Chemical Bank, seconded the motion, and it was clear the other directors agreed. Long rose and left the room without a word.

five

THE MOON SHOT

THE LATE 1960S MAY HAVE BEEN a time of terrible turmoil on earth—assassinations, political upheaval, race riots, the war in Vietnam—but the heavens seemed to offer some solace when Apollo 11 made its triumphant landing on the moon on July 20, 1969. In a world of so many uncertainties, with the nation's institutions under siege, science seemed reassuring in its ability to take the prosaic routines of research and deliver the poetry of success.

Surely, many felt, the technological prowess that allowed the National Aeronautics and Space Administration to safely place two men and their happy four-wheel runabout in the Sea of Tranquility could be applied to other great scientific challenges. At the top of the list was cancer.

It may be hard to imagine today, but the disease was so feared that in some instances, doctors did not even tell patients directly when they had been diagnosed with cancer. Patients, and their families, understood they had severe illnesses, but doctors at times felt they were sparing the patients an unnecessary psychological shock by not uttering the word *cancer*. But now it was smart politics to confront that fear. Science, blind faith, and presidential politics were coming into alignment for a campaign to overcome this threat, once and for all.

Five months after the moon landing, Mary Lasker, a respected health care advocate who had made the fight against cancer her life's mission, and Dr. Sidney Farber, a Harvard oncologist, created the Citizens Committee for the Conquest of Cancer. Lasker was a Washington insider who had spent years cultivating politicians, and she used her prestige and credibility to press her lobbying campaign. Seizing the moment, she and her committee placed a full-page advertisement in the *New York Times* in December 1969 headlined "Mr. Nixon: You Can Cure Cancer." "This year, Mr. President, you have it in your power to begin to end this curse," ran the copy. "America can do this." A cure should be achieved by the bicentennial, in 1976, just seven years away. (That did not seem unreasonable: after President Kennedy's famous declaration that America should put a man on the moon, it had taken eight years to get to the Sea of Tranquility.)

Behind the advertisement was the belief that, like the moon landing, all that stood between the medical com munity and a cure were money and a single-minded focus on discovering new therapies for cancers. With adequate funding and great science, the president could "get this thing done," the ad said, as though it were little more than a question of grit and implementation. (That President Johnson had awarded Lasker the Presidential Medal of Freedom in January 1969 only boosted her credibility.)

But "this thing," the control and cure of cancers, had been defying the best efforts of doctors and scientists for centuries, outwitting the empirical methods used successfully for combating many other diseases. Cancer taxed medical thinking as no illness ever had because it is unlike any other malady.

By 1970 remarkable, if early, progress was being made in unraveling the biology of normal cells. The science was brilliant, but an understanding of the abnormalities in cancer cells was only at the nascent stage; we had few clues as to how to develop effective new cancer treatments. But yet for those at the front lines of research, the cell was yielding its secrets. As Albert Claude described it in his Nobel acceptance speech a few years later, "We have entered the cell, the mansion of our birth, and started the inventory of our acquired wealth."

Lasker proved remarkably effective in winning support for a focused battle against cancer, but her efforts created a tension at the heart of the plan that has never completely gone away: whether funds should be devoted mostly to basic scientific research, to improve our understanding of the biology of cancer, or to programs targeting "the cure," no matter how many enigmas we have yet to solve about cancer's devious behavior.

Such questions were steamrollered, at least initially. A resolution offered in the House of Representatives in March 1970 stated: "That it is the sense of the Congress that the conquest of cancer is a national crusade to be accomplished by 1976. That the Congress appropriate the funds necessary for a massive program of cancer research and for the buildings and equipment . . . so that the citizens of this land and of all other lands may be delivered from the greatest scourge in history."

The Senate followed in late April with a resolution that created a panel of consultants to the conquest of cancer. It consisted of eminent doctors and scientists as well as businessmen and civic leaders who would build support and momentum for the cancer research program. In an effort to be evenhanded, the panel, which Lasker was helping choose, would include both Republicans and Democrats. In picking appropriate Republican candidates, Mrs. Lasker turned to another influential anticancer advocate, Laurance S. Rockefeller, the grandson of John D. Rockefeller and chairman of the board of one of his family's more important philanthropic commitments, the Memorial Sloan-Kettering Cancer Center. Rockefeller agreed to join the panel and recommended Benno C. Schmidt Sr., a Texas-born lawyer and venture capitalist who was also vice chairman of the Memorial Sloan-Kettering board, to serve as its chairman. The panel was given until October, just six months, to formulate a blueprint for an assault on the disease. It did not take long for the committee to confront the central question in the campaign, whether the research should only target developing cures from existing leads or whether scientists should be allowed to explore the basic science behind cancer, in the hopes that doing so would reveal promising avenues for new therapies as part of a longer-term effort.

Those were two sometimes opposing approaches to the development of new treatments, the empirical method and the mechanistic method. In the empirical approach, which defined the way medical research had been conducted for centuries, the development of a drug or other treatment began with observations of known agents. If a plant or chemical or other agent appeared to show some therapeutic benefits, then efforts were directed at improving or refining its properties. This, for example, was how inoculations for some infectious diseases were developed. It is how penicillin was discovered. The experts who developed these important treatments often had no clear understanding of why they worked at the molecular level, but that did not prevent some successes.

The mechanistic approach is fundamentally different. The researcher first develops an understanding of the basic biological mechanisms by which a disease works and uses that to create a customized drug that targets the cellular problem or abnormality behind the illness. If successful, the researchers understand why and how the drug works and often can apply that knowledge to develop more effective drugs for related illnesses or mutations of the disease.

This approach was used for the development of the important anticancer drug Gleevec, which was formulated to attack a relatively rare cancer, chronic myelogenous leukemia, or CML. It was an arduous process. In 1960 two researchers, Peter Nowell, at the University of Pennsylvania, and David Hungerford, at the Fox Chase Cancer Center, discovered a tiny chromosomal abnormality in the leukemia cells of more than 90 percent of the patients with this cancer. They dubbed it the Philadelphia chromosome, after the city where they worked. Thirteen years later, Janet Rowley, a scientist at the University of Chicago, made another breakthrough by determining that the abnormal chromosome was created by the fusion of parts of two normal chromosomes, called chromosome 9 and chromosome 22. A segment of one gene breaks off and fuses with a part of chromosome 22, forming a new gene. This hybrid gene, it was learned years later, carries the code for the synthesis of an enzyme called tyrosine kinase, which supports growth of white blood cells. In healthy cells, this enzyme has a sort of cellular on-off switch, but in the cancer cells, this regulator is, in effect, stuck in the "on" position, leading to runaway growth. Once the scientists understood this cause-and-effect sequence, they were able to identify a chemical that inhibited the enzyme's out-of-control behavior. Using this knowledge, they formulated a drug that put the "switch" in the off position. Gleevec demonstrated that such mechanistic work could be successful, but it took decades and a little luck, and it works only on cancers with that particular genetic "mistake."

The congressional panel tried to paper over the clash between these different research methods. But behind the scenes, numerous scientists and cancer experts expressed concern about several aspects of the emerging battle plans. Should the new government research money be provided in the form of contracts, in which scientists would pursue only specific questions assigned by the central administrators of the federal program? Or would scientists be given grants—the traditional funding method—which would allow them more latitude both in selecting research topics and in shifting the focus in response to their findings?

While advocates of the contract system expected it to be better focused and more productive, the grant system permitted the kind of creativity that good science requires, particularly since so much about the biology of cancer was still not understood. But many of us in the field were growing worried about the direction of the debate.

Robert Marston, the head of the National Institutes of Health, did not believe in targeting cures through contract funding because, put simply, cancer was still so mysterious. As he put it, "The basic lack in the cancer problem is fundamental knowledge of life processes, not developmental capability or central coordination."

The question of how cancer research funds would be allocated was left hanging as President Richard Nixon prepared for his 1971 State of the Union address. Before both houses of Congress in January 1971, he consciously sought to make history with stirring rhetoric and lofty goals. "The time has come in America when the same kind of concentrated effort that split the atom and took man to the moon should be turned toward conquering this dread disease. Let us make a total national commitment to achieve this goal. America has long been the wealthiest nation in the world. Now it is time we became the healthiest nation in the world."

The ambitious proposal was just one of a number of progressive programs Nixon offered in the address. "Tonight I shall present to the Congress six great goals," he announced. "I shall ask not simply for more new programs in the old framework. I shall ask to change the framework of government itself—to reform the entire structure of American government so we can make it again fully responsive to the needs and the wishes of the American people."

Nixon sounded more Democratic than Republican, by today's standards. His initiatives included welfare reform, with a guaranteed minimum income for families and work requirements; an economic stimulus program to reduce unemployment; programs to clean up the environment and expand national parks; and the provision of more policy responsibility and tax revenues to state and local governments. He also called for something close to universal health care to ensure that poor communities and individuals unable to pay for medical treatment had access to adequate health services.

When he turned to cancer, Nixon was very specific. "I will also ask for an appropriation of an extra $100 million to launch an intensive campaign to find a cure for cancer, and I will ask later for whatever additional funds can effectively be used." He was proposing to nearly double the National Cancer Institute's budget. "This can be the Congress that launched a new era in American medicine."

That was it. The "war" on cancer had begun.

Still, the dispute over the best way to allocate the increased funds did not go away. It just grew more intense. In congressional testimony later in 1971, Salvador Luria, a professor at the Massachusetts Institute of Technology and a Nobel laureate in medicine, argued that the idea that a "moon shot" approach could produce a quick cure was "a self-delusion" and would amount to "a dangerous misleading of the public" because it was scientifically premature.

Luria added that cancer had not even been regarded as a serious research subject until about ten years before, and so the great biology and genetic breakthroughs that had been achieved, while exciting, had yet to yield effective new treatments. He called cancer research, quite appropriately, "an extremely frustrating thing."

Congress left those questions to the experts and gave the president what he requested. On December 23, 1971, Nixon signed the National Cancer Act into law. "I hope in the years ahead we will look back on this action today as the most significant action taken during my administration," he said. National Cancer Institute funding grew from $233 million in fiscal year 1971 to more than $1 billion in 1977 and $5 billion in 2011.

As the National Cancer Institute struggled to formulate its action plan, I was drawn into the debate over strategy. In August 1972, the NCI asked the Institute of Medicine at the National Academy of Sciences to assemble a group of experts to assess its approach, and I was one of eleven people chosen for the review. Our chairman was Lewis Thomas, who had left NYU to become dean of the Yale University School of Medicine. The issue under contention was whether the NCI's effort should focus on cures or basic science and whether there should be central control by the government or a decentralized system that granted greater autonomy to the scientists.

The conclusions in our final report, completed in December 1972, reflected our deep concerns about the damage this well-intentioned "war" might have. "It seems to us a defect of the National Cancer Program Plan that the enormity of our ignorance about cancer receives less emphasis than it merits," the report said.

We focused our most intense criticisms on the effort to have the program controlled by one central source, which we saw as extremely foolish and a prescription for failure. The design needed to be more flexible and open to divergent ideas. "If the Congress and public were to conceive of the National Cancer Program Plan as a total plan designed to mobilize all relevant institutions, professional practitioners and technicians of our society into a coordinated and rationalized 'War on Cancer,' it seems unavoidable that the outcome would be the deepest disillusionment," we said.

We were also worried that the National Cancer Institute was moving too slowly. Our panel reviewed only the institute's strategy because a year after the law was passed, the NCI had still not completed an action plan or detailed implementation proposals. That suggested to us a deep dysfunction in the process.

The NCI had produced a preliminary strategy that described its basic approach. The document included a large picture depicting their aims in the shape of a wheel with spokes. There were seven "objectives" in an inner circle of the wheel and seventy-two "approaches" arranged around the spokes on an outer circle.

We were stunned by the naïveté behind this design. Such a rigid structure would choke off curiosity and prevent fresh ideas from being considered, a major shortcoming given the vast holes in our understanding of the basic biology of cancer. In space exploration, the challenges were mostly technological—we knew how to build rockets to escape earth's gravitational pull, so it was a matter of smart engineers developing the systems to propel and protect the astronauts on their way, not inventing entirely new science. With cancer, we were still trying to comprehend the shape-shifting nature of our foe. The final report, written by Lewis Thomas, expressed our deep concerns that the war on cancer, as designed, threatened to run off the rails before it even got started: "It leaves the impression that all shots can be called from a central headquarters, that all or nearly all of the really important ideas are already in hand, and the hard problems can be solved. It fails to allow for the surprises which must surely lie ahead and if we are really going to gain an understanding of cancer."

It was clear that those allocating the funding did not appreciate that investments in basic science promised breakthroughs in many diseases, not just cancer. As would be borne out again and again over the years, infectious diseases, autoimmune diseases, cardiovascular disease, and metabolic diseases like diabetes all benefited from the molecular biology research we advocated. The payoffs were actually coming earlier in those areas. These included vaccines for viral diseases, antibiotics for infectious diseases, and the development of therapies for some heart illnesses.

We received little in the way of a response from the National Cancer Institute, and I remained unsettled as the government prepared to fund major research projects. At various institutions, scientists were developing profound new insights into the way DNA communicates its instructions, the pathways involved in genetic expression, and why tiny genetic errors can wreak havoc. But we could not yet translate those findings into therapies. In other words, we were at a point of takeoff in the science of genetics and molecular biology, but not in the development of new anticancer drugs. And the principal curative treatment for solid tumors, like breast, prostate, and colon cancers, remained surgery, which was effective only in removing cancers that had not metastasized.

Most forms of chemotherapy provided very temporary remissions. That stood in contrast to the great successes medicine had achieved in fighting other diseases. Vaccines for infectious diseases, such as smallpox, were nearly 100 percent effective. But the best anticancer drugs worked only sporadically, and during those years we often could not accurately predict which patients would benefit and which would not. Some metastatic cancers would go into remission only to come roaring back, yet we frequently could not anticipate when this would happen, or say why.

I began discussing with friends how we could address the problems. First, if researchers failed to deliver the "cures" that Nixon and Congress expected in a relatively short period of time, which would surely be the case, it could undermine public confidence, and the funding we needed to forge ahead in basic science might evaporate.

Worse, the fixation on cures could pressure universities to skew their efforts toward drug development and a quest for "magic bullets" just to win grants. With Columbia receiving a large amount of federal funding for the traditional-style grants for basic research, I feared that our academic mission would be distorted.

I shared my anxieties with my mentor from my days at the National Institutes of Health, Arthur Kornberg, who was then chairman of the Department of Biochemistry at Stanford University. Kornberg had more recently served on the National Cancer Panel, which formulated the recommendations for the National Cancer Act. I was nervous about complaining to the government because we were so dependent on their grant programs, but Kornberg urged me to write to Benno Schmidt Sr., who was the panel's chairman.

Finally, on February 11, 1975, after going through many drafts, I sent a one-page letter to Schmidt explaining that a significant amount of the appropriations should be dedicated to basic research on genetics and molecular biology and that the expectations for the development of "cures," no matter how enticing, should be set low. And I warned against the potentially negative impact on research in universities. "On the one hand, the pressure on many of these institutions to attract National Cancer Institute funding has long term implications for balanced academic programs and consequently for the long term stability and quality of the institutions," I wrote. "I do not present this concern as a 'fault' in the National Cancer Program. Rather I may be sensing a realistic and I believe undesirable by-product."

False hopes could be devastating for our cancer research, which was already facing skepticism. That would be the case for many years, as people waited impatiently for cures in the hope that we could finally reverse the tragically high, and rising, cancer death rates. We were being measured, criticized, and prodded, and this would go on for years. (In 1986, for instance, a fairly typical article in the *New England Journal of Medicine* complained that "we are losing the war against cancer.") At that early stage of the campaign, I wanted a program that would have staying power and that, most important, could achieve long-range success. I got my concerns off my chest and expected nothing in response. I had Columbia and the students to worry about.

Six days later I received a one-paragraph letter from Schmidt. "I think your suggestion is a good one and I will undertake to see the action is instituted along the lines you propose," he said.

Not long after that, he invited me to Washington. I met with the head of the National Cancer Institute to discuss my ideas, and Schmidt recommended that I be appointed to the three-member Presidential Cancer Panel. The panel, which met every other month at the National Cancer Institute in Bethesda, oversaw both the implementation of the National Cancer Act and the institute's other programs. I suddenly found myself at the center of this new war.

six

TEACHING CANCER CELLS TO DIE

A S I WAS CONTENDING WITH the debate over cancer funding in the early 1970s, Charlotte Friend, a professor of microbiology at Mount Sinai Medical School in New York, was experimenting with a virus that caused leukemia in mice by inducing genetic mutations. To better understand the process through which the virus transformed healthy blood cells into abnormal ones, she decided to "superinfect" the blood cells with the virus, that is, to force even more of it into the mouse cells.

To do this, Friend treated the cells with a solvent called dimethyl sulfoxide, or DMSO, that made their membranes more permeable to large molecules. DMSO is a by-product of pulp and paper production that at one time had a reputation for remarkable healing properties when dabbed on the skin. But in 1965 the Food and Drug

Administration (FDA) banned it for human use because there was no proof of its effectiveness, and it was also a member of a class of chemicals, called polar molecules, that are known to be toxic.

The DMSO was merely the first mechanical step in her research, but two or three days after the cells had been treated with the solution, she observed something startling: the mouse leukemia cells, which had been colorless before being treated, were tinted pink and red.

In my own research at Columbia, I had continued my investigation into the regulation of the expression of globin genes in red blood cells, and I had been publishing papers about my findings. Globin or, more accurately, hemoglobin is the vital protein in red blood cells that takes up oxygen when the cells circulate through our lungs. When hemoglobin is formed, an iron molecule is inserted into the globin protein, giving it its distinctive red color. Friend, having read some of my papers, called me to discuss her observations of the DMSO experiment. She got right to the point.

"What human proteins are red?" she asked.

I answered, "There's only one."

I told her it was hemoglobin. What Friend had discovered was that DMSO had, in effect, switched on a genetic function in the leukemic mouse blood cells that the disease had switched off. That is how the DMSO had induced the infected mouse leukemia cells to produce hemoglobin.

It was as though they had gone from sick to healthy. This was new. She reported her findings in the *Proceedings of the National Academy of Sciences,* in 1971, and in her paper "Hemoglobin Synthesis in Murine Virus-Induced Leukemic Cells *in Vitro*: Stimulation of Erythroid Differentiation by Dimethyl Sulfoxide," she offered a theory about the surprising reaction. "This action of dimethyl sulfoxide, which was reversible, may represent the derepression of leukemic cells to permit their maturation."

I wondered whether this fascinating accident might further my studies into how the expression of globin genes is controlled within cells. I asked Friend if she could share some mouse leukemia cells and DMSO so I could reproduce her experiment. She invited me to her laboratory at Mount Sinai Hospital at Madison Avenue and East 101st Street to collect the samples.

This was the essence of serious science: having a plan and a goal, but being willing to alter it at any time because of new information. Scientists need to be not just receptive when an interesting accident happens, but ready to exploit the opening and tease out the meaning of the unexpected phenomenon. Study, planning, and discipline are critical, but the best scientists can improvise when the unexpected takes over. As Nobel laureate Peter Medawar wrote, "The prepared mind is essential to good science." Sometimes the unexpected is a path to failure, but at others it can be a gateway to discovery.

Excitedly, I returned to my lab with Friend's samples and treated the mouse cells with the DMSO. I waited. Nothing happened. The test tubes with the mouse leukemia cells did not turn red. I repeated the procedure, but the DMSO was not working. I had no choice but to call Friend and acknowledge my failure. She said she knew.

Scientists are human, and it turned out she had given me the wrong cells. I chalked it up to paranoia about my intentions, a test of sorts on her part. But she agreed to provide the correct sample, and I was soon staring into a test tube tinted red; about two-thirds of the cancer cells were suddenly in living color. I was awed. It was like looking at a sort of biological crop circle—this was either a pretty but meaningless curiosity or a profound, if opaque, message from deep inside our cells.

That, it turned out, was just the start. Observing the red-tinted cells in a test tube a few days later, I was at first mystified and then struck by another observation. The DMSO had not just induced a moribund cellular function to snap into action, but also stopped the cancer cells from growing. Leukemia causes blood cells to multiply madly out of control, but DMSO had brought the process to a halt in all the treated samples.

I turned over the possibility in my mind. Was I looking at a potential treatment for cancer?

After decades of painstaking science, by the early 1970s we were beginning to understand the behavior of cancer

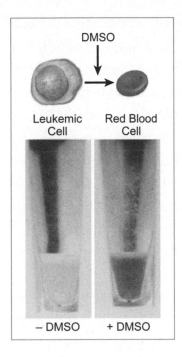

Leukemic Cell   Red Blood Cell

− DMSO   + DMSO

Charlotte Friend discovered that adding the solvent DMSO to a test tube of mouse leukemia cells spurred the production of hemoglobin. The test tube went from clear to red.

cells at the most fundamental level. A normal cell undergoes a genetic mutation or, more often, several mutations that transform it from a cog in the biological machine of the body, performing some small but critical task, into a serial killer. The transformation disrupts the normal processes that regulate cell behavior, and the cancer cells divide out of control, refuse to die, and then gain mobility and the ability to flow into other parts of the body, destroying healthy tissue and organs. But we still knew almost nothing about how to manipulate or reverse those lethal genetic insurgencies.

I had been focusing on relatively narrow questions about the ways that genes express their coded information in red blood cells. I had not yet approached cancer directly because of its immense complexity. I was contributing, I believed, to building a foundation for understanding the ways cancers work. But now things seemed to have leaped ahead. The potential implications of my test tube of mouse blood cells were unmistakable: I was looking at a chemical that coaxed the monster back into a benign state and, even better, did not appear to endanger healthy cells.

Chemically, DMSO is a simple molecule, represented schematically as:

Polar methyl

$$^-O = S\text{-}(CH_3)_2$$

On the left is an oxygen molecule (O), which makes up what is known as a "polar group," linked to a sulfur molecule (S). Polar groups are chemically reactive and in normal processes are known to attach to various molecules in the body. On the right side of the DMSO molecule, the sulfur is linked to two methyl groups $(CH_3)_2$, which can also be involved in various metabolic reactions in healthy cells. So our first challenge was determining which side of the DMSO molecule, the polar group or the methyl group, was stopping the growth of cancer cells.

We conducted the obvious tests on the mouse leukemia cells, first substituting other compounds for the DMSO that acted as methyl donors. None worked. But when we substituted chemical compounds that were polar, the growth of the leukemia cells was stopped cold, leading us to conclude that our target was some kind of polar molecule. Because an industrial solvent like DMSO is too toxic to use in humans, we had to find a safe polar compound that produced the same results.

I pored over a long list of polar chemicals, but I was a medical doctor steeped in molecular biology—the names meant nothing to me. Working with my colleagues who had some background in chemistry, we chose a dozen and ordered them from a supply house. Like magic, all the polar compounds induced the mouse leukemia cells to produce hemoglobin and to stop growing. (I explained these results in a paper published in a scientific journal in 1975. But the phenomenon was so complex that it would take us another twenty years to figure out that the polar compounds worked by blocking enzymes called histone deacetylases.) These were promising insights, but we were still in the dark on the ultimate test, whether the polar compounds could stop cancerous growths in humans.

We did not let this delay our search for what might be a powerful anticancer drug, and we moved on to the challenge of finding a different polar chemical that could be tolerated in humans. I called my friend Roy Vagelos, head of research at Merck, told him of my findings, and asked if he could give me a small sample of polar chemicals that they had in their drug-development pipeline. I was hoping that the chemists at Merck had made something that would have the effect of DMSO without negative side effects. Roy generously arranged to send me about two hundred compounds, though he kept the proprietary chemical formulas confidential. None had the effect of DMSO.

But another happy accident opened the door to more effective approaches. A talented postdoctoral fellow in my laboratory, Roberta Rubin, had previously done a fellowship with Columbia chemistry professor Ronald Breslow, and she suggested that we consult with him. He was immediately intrigued, starting a collaboration that has lasted more than three decades. After I explained our findings, he sketched out the structure of several polar compounds on his blackboard. If one polar group on a chemical like DMSO was good, he argued, two might be better. So he proposed fabricating compounds with polar groups at both ends, separated by anywhere from one to eight carbon molecules (C), and then testing them one at a time.

We determined in the lab that the optimal effect was obtained with a compound in which the two polar groups were separated by six carbon (C_6) atoms. The chemical was called hexamethylene bisacetamide, or HMBA. It was fifty times more active than DMSO in turning the mouse leukemia cells red, and it was not toxic to normal cells in a test tube.

The next step was to begin testing HMBA on various cancer cells in test tubes. We obtained more than sixty different human cancer cell lines that were kept at the National Cancer Institute precisely for the sort of experiment we were

---

HMBA

Hexamethylene bis(acetamide)

In refining the DMSO solvent, we found the optimal anti-cancer benefits came from a chemical compound in which two polar groups were separated by six carbon atoms, called HMBA.

conducting. The HMBA arrested the growth in those human cancer cells as well. We were excited by the promise of what we had found and thought we were closing in on an understanding of how these compounds stopped cancers.

The real question, of course, was how the chemical would work outside of test tubes. Would HMBA stop a human tumor from growing? We decided to take the first preliminary step toward finding out: we would try the HMBA in live mice with the experimentally induced leukemia. The efforts failed. The drug had no therapeutic effect on the leukemia; the mice died in six to eight weeks whether or not they received HMBA.

In an article we wrote in 1979 for the *Annual Review of Biochemistry,* we described how we had found a potentially "new and provocative mechanism" for arresting cancer but acknowledged that the mechanism by which it worked was a mystery. We also did not understand why the HMBA worked in test tubes but failed in stopping the cancer in mice.

We had run into the inscrutability and evasiveness of the disease. Each new problem we faced had led to a string of new molecular conundrums that taxed our scientific understanding of the cell. But by 1980 we knew that we had stopped the unlimited proliferation of cancer cells in test tubes with a chemical that did not kill healthy cells. It was a start.

seven

THE POLITICS OF CANCER RESEARCH

V IRUSES ARE LITTLE MORE THAN primitive, if crafty, bundles of genetic material in protein sheaths—molecular drones that "bomb" cells with their infectious payloads—so the discovery of how they can cause cancers opened the way to a number of important insights in the 1970s. Once specific viruses had been identified as cancer-causing agents, such as hepatitis B, which can induce liver damage and ultimately lead to liver cancer, work began on vaccines to reduce the spread of the diseases. Roughly 20 percent of cancers may be caused by viruses. Those were important steps in the battle to prevent some cancers during the early days of the campaign, but to broaden our attacks, researchers still had to grapple with the complex fundamentals of cellular behavior and the many ways normal cells are transformed into cancer cells.

We knew that some of the viruses that can induce cancer contain strands of DNA inside the protein sheaths. That suggested that this genetic software, once inserted into the host cells, sends out encoded instructions that cause abnormal cell growth. That is how viral DNA can turn healthy cells into malignant cells.

But during the 1970s, a startling finding challenged that model: one virus known to cause cancer—the HTLV-1 virus, which can induce T-cell leukemia—contains no DNA. Instead, it contains RNA. It was thought at that time that RNA was a mere transmitter of genetic instructions, a messenger, rather than a repository of those instructions. Discovering a virus that contained only RNA was a little like discovering a functioning automobile with a transmission but no engine.

Up to that time, it was believed that the messenger process went only one way, from the DNA, the master genetic-software blueprint, to the messenger RNA as the communication agent. The RNA then took the information to the area of the cell where new proteins are manufactured and put these genetic instructions to work.

DNA → RNA → Protein Synthesis

But if a virus that contained only RNA was causing lethal changes in the proteins, and DNA, of healthy cells, the process, it seemed, had to be able to move in the opposite direction as well; the messenger was, in effect, creating the master software rather than just transmitting its messages. These viruses were named retroviruses, because the RNA essentially works in reverse. (The HIV virus, which causes AIDS, is probably the best-known retrovirus.) They rely on an enzyme called reverse transcriptase to produce new DNA from their RNA; the DNA is then incorporated into the genes of the healthy cells, creating the cancerous mutations.

David Baltimore, Renato Dulbecco, and Howard Temin won the Nobel Prize in Medicine in 1975 for their remarkable discovery of reverse transcriptase.

There was a double-edged message behind this breakthrough: scientists had discovered not just an important new method by which cells communicate information but how little we still knew about the ways that cancerous cells are created. Nevertheless, those early years in the war on cancer were exciting and productive. Scientists delved deep into the molecular mechanisms of normal and cancer cells and unraveled many of their mysteries.

Michael Bishop and Harold Varmus (Varmus had been a student of mine at Columbia) later showed that the cancer-causing genes of animal retroviruses are actually derived from normal cellular genes, which are present in virtually all animals, including human beings. These cellular genes, they found, were mutated in most human cancers. The proteins they make became the targets for many new kinds of cancer treatments. Bishop and Varmus were awarded a Nobel Prize, in 1989, for their discovery.

Not long after, Harald zur Hausen, a German researcher, showed that the human papillomavirus may be a cause of cervical cancer in women, another important breakthrough that allowed scientists to develop a preventive vaccine for cervical cancer. Harald zur Hausen was awarded a Nobel Prize in 2008.

These findings also made clear that more investment in basic science and molecular biology would be required if we were to have any hope of developing better cancer treatments. Unfortunately, it was not certain that the federal government and public advocacy groups had that kind of patience.

The policy makers, still mesmerized by the "moon shot" analogy, wanted a cure sooner rather than later. They had little interest in the tantalizing biological questions that had to be answered—or a process that could take years. We were fighting both a medical war and a Washington-style funding battle.

As a follow-up to Nixon's war on cancer legislation, the White House created a panel of scientists in January 1975 to chart a comprehensive national strategy for biomedical research. This was intended to be a massive effort to identify appropriate research and funding priorities. I was one of seven people selected to serve on the panel, which was chaired by Franklin Murphy, chairman of the Times Mirror

Corporation (then the owner of the *Los Angeles Times*), the former chancellor of the University of California at Los Angeles, and a medical doctor by training.

We were sworn in by Vice President Nelson Rockefeller in his office in the old State Department building next to the White House, with the secretary of health, education, and welfare (HEW), Caspar Weinberger, looking on. We had just eighteen months to devise the plan. We quickly got down to work, gathering the vast amount of information needed to make smart recommendations and commissioning reports from academic experts and biomedical think tanks on the state of research.

Important as it was, this was not a high-profile project in the eyes of many important people in Washington. Few in the public and, perhaps, even in government were aware of the panel's work or the significance it could have for cancer research and biomedical studies.

Our staff assembled and refined the data, which was then organized into a strategy for each area of research and drug development. The report provided an authoritative synthesis of the then current knowledge in the biomedical sciences and medicine. Our panel agreed that large-scale federal support for basic biomedical science was "the only sound basis for learning how to prevent and control diseases."

Beneath our evenhanded estimates of the future, we had adopted a slightly pugnacious tone. We urged that the federal government support basic scientific research, under the direction of the National Institutes of Health, and not throw too much money at the false promise of quick cures for cancer or other diseases. "A vigorous program of fundamental research in all institutes is essential to the continuing strength of the biomedical research effort," we said. But we also warned that if the NIH became a service agency, merely trying to translate science into cures, "one of the world's greatest scientific resources will be placed in jeopardy."

Our ideas were tested in May 1976 at congressional hearings chaired by Senator Edward Kennedy. The members of the committee applauded our report, but, behind the scenes, government officials grumbled that it had not included concrete steps that would lead to a range of cures for major diseases. The *Wall Street Journal* reported on May 3, 1976, that "some HEW officials privately are not hiding their disappointment with the Murphy panel's product. They view it as self-serving." Their concern, and that of "some congressmen," was that our panel emphasized the importance of basic research and not federal support for "activities more relevant to current medical care concerns." The politics had gotten way ahead of the science.

This was a replay of the argument that broke out—after the National Cancer Act of 1971 was passed—between scientists, like myself, and Mary Lasker and her citizens' committee. In spite of the scientific progress we had made, we still did not have the fundamental knowledge needed to treat many conditions. These included not just cancer, but also mental disorders and certain types of heart disease. In many instances, we were groping in the dark, and our panel did not want to pretend otherwise.

By the time our panel's report was completed, in April 1976, the criticisms had taken their toll. The biomedical report, though comprehensive and, I believed, farsighted, was buried, and the opportunity to set a national strategy for biomedical research was lost. The spending now is hostage to whatever health issues the political parties think are important at any point in time.

The experience was frustrating, but it underscored the reality that curing cancer was as much a political as a medical mission. It felt like we had to get not one thing right, but everything right, if we were to succeed.

The United States was not the only country where politics, and even corruption, played a significant role in determining the course of medical research, of course. This was driven home for me when I was asked by the Iranian government to help the country build a world-class medical center. This misadventure began in December 1974, when I received a letter unexpectedly inviting me to travel to Teheran to meet with the shah of Iran and offer advice on building a modern medical school and a major cancer center.

Columbia University's president, William McGill, and I flew to Iran in December. When we arrived, we were whisked through passport control and driven to a luxury hotel. Our suite was amply stocked with champagne and caviar and had a lovely view of the snowcapped mountains to the north.

The next day we were driven to the palace. We were received by the shah, who explained that he wanted to construct a major new health center both to train more doctors and to attract Iranian expatriates back home to assist with the country's development. At the shah's request, I agreed to organize a group of leaders from several other US medical schools—Harvard, Cornell, Chicago, and the University of California, San Francisco—and develop a curriculum and plan for the new school and the clinical facilities. It seemed like a worthy project, and the Iranian people certainly needed better health care.

Not long afterward, I was told the advisory committee I had organized would report directly to Princess Ashraf Pahlavi, the shah's twin sister. It was not a good sign. During a visit in 1976, she invited me to dinner at her palace, and in the course of the conversation she explained that I was obliged to direct a significant portion of the budget being provided by the government directly to her to "facilitate" the medical program. In a subsequent meeting with the Health Ministry, we were told that further portions of our budget had to be kicked back to the minister's office.

Later, when I asked if I could tour the countryside and get a feel for Iran's rural areas, I was confronted with another obstacle. Some of the villages I saw were poor, with no electricity or running water, and the clerics—the village leaders—made it clear that they would fight the development of the medical school and its clinical facilities. They were adamantly opposed to offering instruction in English, and they refused to accept our plan to open the school to women as well as men. The clerics also said that they would resist any program supported by the shah because of their hatred for the monarchy.

In January 1979, before plans for the school or cancer center could move forward, the Iranian revolution overthrew the shah's government, and he was forced into exile. He died in 1980—from cancer. It was yet another lesson in the reality that science never operates in a vacuum.

eight

MEMORIAL SLOAN-KETTERING FINDS ITS AGENT OF CHANGE

"DO YOU KNOW WHO WON the Heisman Trophy last year?"

I paused at the question, but, given that the governor of Texas was asking, I had to assume he was serious. I had no idea who had won that football trophy in 1977, but it was clearly a point of Texas pride. It wasn't worth guessing.

"You know, I can't seem to recall," I said, "but he must have been quite a player."

The governor, Dolph Briscoe, was interviewing me for the job of president of the MD Anderson Cancer Center in Houston, but his dismay seemed to match mine when I was forced to plead ignorance. He tried to sound enthusiastic when he told me the trophy had been won by Earl Campbell, the great running back from the University of Texas, but it felt like some of the air had gone out of the room. He clearly did not see me as the sort of Texas booster he was hoping to place at the head of this excellent medical institution. I regarded it as the second-best cancer center in the country—after Memorial Sloan-Kettering in New York.

But I had other concerns about this job that went beyond issues of sports trivia; they had to do with my continuing frustrations in developing a major cancer center at Columbia's medical school, where I was vice president. I was concerned that MD Anderson, like Columbia, took too narrow an approach to basic scientific research.

Some of our best medical institutions were, I felt, too balkanized to produce the most effective marriage of clinical programs and research efforts. Three years before getting the call from MD Anderson, I had struggled to overcome these shortcomings at Columbia and still felt some resistance toward developing a broad and deep cancer program.

As planned, I had stepped down in 1973 as dean of the medical school after three years, but Columbia's president, William McGill, had persuaded me to continue in an administrative role as vice president for health sciences, a newly created position. The job allowed me to conduct my research with only light administrative duties. More important, I was able to organize an effort to build up Columbia's cancer research efforts and mount a campaign to earn for the school status as a government-recognized "comprehensive cancer center."

That designation was an important provision of the National Cancer Act of 1971. They were to be distinguished by scientific excellence and a diverse range of research programs focused on cancer. The goal was to attack cancer through integrated programs in laboratory research, innovative clinical trials, and prevention research.

In early 1972, the National Cancer Institute initially designated the first three centers: Memorial Sloan-Kettering Cancer Center in New York City, MD Anderson Cancer Center in Houston, and Roswell Park Cancer Institute in Buffalo, New York. By 1974 a number of others were added, including the Dana-Farber Cancer Institute in Boston, the University of Chicago Comprehensive Cancer Center in Chicago, and the Sidney Kimmel Comprehensive Cancer Center at Johns Hopkins University in Baltimore. Today there are forty-one designated centers in twenty-three states and the District of Columbia.

Our basic cancer research program at Columbia was strong, with the laboratories at the Francis Delafield Hospital. Several of our faculty members in the basic science departments were engaged in excellent research programs. However, due to New York City's fiscal crisis, the local government was preparing to close Delafield, along with its research labs. We turned to the National Cancer Institute to fund new facilities, but they could contribute only if the medical center had been designated a "comprehensive" cancer center.

We had to prepare to apply for the designation, but up to that time, the mid-1970s, Columbia-Presbyterian's clinical cancer program did little original research. It participated in few cancer drug trials or evaluations of new approaches to cancer diagnosis and early detection. In truth, the clinical departments—medicine, surgery, pediatrics, and obstetrics and gynecology—had no dedicated oncology group. Sixty percent of our cancer patients had a form of the disease that was not amenable to surgery, but fewer than 3 percent of those were entered in "innovative clinical anticancer drug trials." The NCI required a far greater commitment before it would consider providing funding for a new building and give the Columbia-Presbyterian Medical Center the "comprehensive cancer center" designation.

A number of institutional hurdles contributed to the lagging pace of Columbia-Presbyterian's cancer care. For one thing, the hospital's physicians were predominantly in private practice. They were not staff members with a full-time commitment to the hospital or the medical school. Caring for patients with cancer, particularly patients with inoperable cancer, was extremely complex, time-consuming, and frustrating. In short, it was medically challenging and not financially rewarding relative to the time required. This was particularly true for cancer patients in clinical trials, which requires even more paperwork, monitoring, and follow-up. It was not a moneymaker and so was not attractive to most doctors in private practice.

I finally persuaded the chairmen of the clinical departments to recruit cancer specialists to bolster our application to the NCI and to improve research. We eventually succeeded, in 1976, in winning the "comprehensive cancer center" designation, and that allowed us to obtain the funding needed for constructing the new research laboratory building.

It was progress, but there was still a resistant culture at Columbia that I could not entirely overcome. Even with the changes, the clinical departments did not embrace oncology and cancer treatment as major priorities, I felt, and, as a result, the quality of our care was not as good as I hoped. We never took a leading role in developing new anticancer drugs or therapies.

The basic scientific research programs were flourishing; investigators were exploring the role of viruses in inducing cancers, environmental hazards, immunological approaches to cancer therapy, the development of new diagnostic tests, and new anticancer drugs. But we had no beds in the clinical facilities for trials or clinical oncologists committed to the research program. It felt like we were coasting, so when I got the call from MD Anderson in 1979 sounding me out on the job as president, I was receptive.

I had learned useful lessons in how to organize a program to achieve progress in our still young war on cancer.

Perhaps, I thought, I could put these ideas into practice in Houston. My initial contact at MD Anderson was R. Lee Clark, the outgoing president who had served with me on the President's Cancer Panel. We started our conversation by discussing future plans for the center, and I quickly found we had real differences.

My view was that because of the enormous complexities in the biology of cancer and the breadth of scientific knowledge required both to understand and to develop treatments, all the scientific and medical disciplines had to work closely together, from patient care to basic research. As I had learned from my efforts to develop an effective anticancer drug from DMSO, you never knew where promising ideas might come from: an industrial solvent might open a door. Clark, on the other hand, believed that everyone at MD Anderson had to be directly engaged in cancer research with an emphasis on developing new treatments. To me, that was limiting, and I said so.

I explained that I had spent years researching thalassemia, the genetic blood disorder. I acknowledged that it was not a type of cancer—in fact, at the time, I did not have a single cancer cell in my lab—but I believed that what I was learning about the behavior of genes, enzymes, and gene expression was applicable to cancer treatments. But Clark felt that an overly liberal interpretation of what constituted cancer research would distract from MD Anderson's real purpose.

This dispute and the jarring experience of the Heisman Trophy quiz left me unsettled, so when I returned to New York, I consulted with a friend I had come to know well, Benno Schmidt. He was a Texan, so I thought he would be a useful sounding board.

After I explained my dilemma—frustration at Columbia but concerns about the single-minded focus at MD Anderson—Schmidt waved me off. "You know, I'm from Texas, and I can tell you, you won't last there," he said. "You wouldn't be able to deal with Texas politics." Then he said something cryptic that barely registered with me at the time. "I've got a different job in mind for you."

I felt stuck, both personally and as an "officer" in this medical "war." We had made progress in understanding cancer biology, but translating that into therapies was lagging at Columbia, as it was at most medical schools.

It was known by then that cancer involved gene mutations and that certain normal genes could be converted into "oncogenes," by viruses or other means, which induced malignancies. We had also identified special protective genes that suppressed cancer growth, and these "suppressors" could be switched off, allowing cancers to blossom and spread unobstructed. Recently, researchers have identified seventy suppressor genes and forty-seven oncogenes in an analysis of many different cancers.

Clinically, surgery remained the principal potentially curative therapy for solid tumors, as long as they were localized. Once they had metastasized, we could offer drugs or radiation treatment to buy some time. Anticancer drugs were generally administered as cocktails of two to four different agents. Each was believed to hit a different target in the cancer cells, but we understood little about what those targets were and why the drugs worked, when they did. Nor did we understand exactly why they stopped working, which was often the case.

We had slightly better treatments for "liquid" tumors, such as lymphomas and leukemia, with chemotherapy and radiation. But by 1980 an effective new anticancer agent had not reached the market in several years. The oncology field needed to become more creative.

I was restless, but I turned down the MD Anderson job and put it out of my mind. That fall Schmidt invited me and my wife, Joan, over for dinner. We had been to his home before and enjoyed his company. This time we walked in to find Laurance Rockefeller, the chairman of the board of the Memorial Sloan-Kettering Cancer Center, among the small group gathered for the evening. It was my first encounter with a man who would become a close friend and a critical influence on my career.

Over a cocktail hour that went on for some time, as was usual at the Schmidts', Joan and Laurance moved to a corner of the living room and plunged into a long and intimate conversation. He was soon sharing with her personal concerns about the anxieties of parenting in a new, free-spirited era.

Joan, ever the social worker, offered him some comforting family advice, and he seemed to appreciate the suggestions. He was clearly fond of her and took her warmth to heart.

(He also had his oddities. The first time my wife, Joan, and I had dinner at his home with him and his wife, Mary, Laurance gave us a tour of his remarkable art collection. "You don't realize it, I don't even think Mary realizes it, but these are all copies," he said of the paintings around us by Renoir, Matisse, Homer, and other masters. "I had the originals copied so we could place them in museums." Each copy was exactly one inch larger than the genuine articles so they would not be confused. When I became president of the cancer center, his brother Nelson lent a beautiful Matisse, *The Italian Woman,* to hang in my office. Laurance visited and said that it, too, would be copied. The original is now in the collection of the Guggenheim Museum in New York.)

It was a pleasant evening and flattering to socialize with a Rockefeller, but in the weeks that followed we thought little about it. Then, shortly before Christmas, my assistant, Joyce Stichman, interrupted me one afternoon to say I had an important call. I answered to find Laurance Rockefeller on the line. He was cordial but wasted little time in getting to the point. One of his close associates, Harold Helm, the former chairman of Chemical Bank and a trustee of Columbia-Presbyterian Hospital, had recommended me as a candidate for president of the Memorial Sloan-Kettering Cancer Center, he said. Was I interested?

The Rockefeller family took their philanthropy very seriously. John D. Rockefeller Jr., Laurance's father, had assigned key institutions to each of his children and expected them to shepherd them with purpose and energy. Laurance was assigned Memorial Sloan-Kettering. It was an emotional favorite of his father's—a privately published family history describes how his grief over the loss of a close childhood friend, a vivacious young woman, after a battle with cancer fired John D. Rockefeller Jr.'s commitment to conquering the disease.

The original Memorial Hospital had opened on Manhattan's Upper West Side in 1884 as the New York Cancer Hospital, the country's first devoted solely to cancer care. It excelled in surgery, but was also a leader in developing drugs and techniques for using radiation to treat cancer. In 1939 it moved to the East Side, on land donated by John D. Rockefeller Jr., across York Avenue from Rockefeller University and Cornell Medical School. Rockefeller's intention was that Memorial's association with these other institutions would improve its programs, making it an incubator of cutting-edge cancer research and cancer treatments. The Sloan-Kettering Institute was added in 1945, named for the two General Motors executives who helped fund it—Alfred P. Sloan, the auto company's chairman for many years, and Charles F. Kettering, the head of research at GM.

But by the late 1970s, Laurance had lost confidence in the cancer center's chief of research, Dr. Robert Good, in the wake of a laboratory scandal involving a doctor who falsified research. In our conversations, he only hinted at his concerns, but Memorial Sloan-Kettering was producing no great breakthroughs in cancer treatment, which was the purpose of the institution. Surgery remained the primary treatment for cancer patients with potentially curable tumors, including breast, prostate, colon, and lung cancers. Dr. Edward Beattie, the head of the hospital and a highly skilled surgeon, regarded chemotherapy and radiotherapy as a recourse only if surgery was not an option or had failed. Memorial Sloan-Kettering was part of a cancer-treatment complex that was falling behind in the effort to turn great science into better therapies, and Rockefeller knew it.

Also in the background motivating Laurance were comparisons to his brother David. Though Laurance never admitted it openly to me, he hinted from time to time that he feared he was losing a rivalry with his brother, who was chairman of the board of Rockefeller University, the medical-research powerhouse located just across the street. The university's prestige soared as its researchers broke new ground in a variety of fields; Memorial Sloan-Kettering, on the other hand, had developed into a very good hospital for cancer surgery. Something had to be done.

Rockefeller and Benno Schmidt had been talking for some time about both reorganizing Memorial Sloan-Kettering and finding a new leader to change the culture. I was enormously flattered when Rockefeller called. He made it clear that he was not looking for a mere adminis-trator or a steward but wanted a new vision and forceful leadership. Moreover, he felt it was time to unify the sepa-rate halves of the center.

Memorial Hospital and the Sloan-Kettering Institute were loosely affiliated, with separate boards and separate budgets and a small umbrella organization above them that held little real power. Laurance's idea was to empower this body as a way of unifying and coordinating the clinical and research efforts. He believed better and closer coopera-tion would generate more progress. Given my frustrations at Columbia with the rifts between the hospital and the medical school, I understood his concerns.

I was enthusiastic, but from the start friends warned me that I faced an uphill struggle. Great as its reputation was within the worlds of medicine and research, Memo-rial Sloan-Kettering in 1980 was not at the cutting edge in cancer research. I took advantage of a gathering at the National Academy of Sciences to ask a good friend, Baruj Benacerraf, the director of the Dana-Farber Cancer Institute in Boston, how the idea struck him. He all but laughed. "You're absolutely out of your mind," he warned me. Me-morial Sloan-Kettering's hospital in those days was basi-cally a surgical hospital, albeit a good one, he said, known for "heavy cutting." It had fallen behind in promising ar-eas like genetics and molecular biology and, clinically, in radiotherapy and medical oncology. "Do you think you're going to recruit anybody who isn't a surgeon?" Benacerraf asked. "Get out!" (I would later learn that the board had approached Benacerraf about the president's job, but he had declined.)

When I visited with Beattie for the first time as a candidate for president, he took me on a tour of the operating rooms, but did not introduce me to any other doctors or show me other parts of the hospital, as though they hardly mattered. If I was offered the job, I thought, I had a mountain to climb to build up Memorial Sloan-Kettering's research departments.

During long interviews with Rockefeller and the Board of Trustees, I spelled out my belief that Memorial Sloan-Kettering needed a major recruiting drive to attract the absolute best clinicians and researchers. The current staff also needed to be thoroughly assessed, and, when necessary, some would be let go. I explained that more funding would be required for research programs in genetics and molecular biology and clinical programs in radiotherapy and medical oncology.

In early-March 1980, Rockefeller called and offered me the position as the first president and chief executive officer of a unified Memorial Sloan-Kettering Cancer Center (MSKCC). In a seven-page, single-spaced letter, I accepted the position and again explained my vision, to forewarn the board that some turmoil might be coming. For me, this was about adding new vitality not just to this wonderful institution but to the national battle against cancer, which risked stagnation. Memorial Sloan-Kettering was a microcosm of that effort to advance cancer research and cancer care. I wrote, "The single most important issue facing MSKCC is developing a process for the review of the quality of programs and staff to achieve the goals of excellence. Such an initiative would have my highest priority. Programs identified as weak or low priority would be phased out, a process that could involve a considerable turnover of existing scientific staff."

I stopped short of stating that I would push for construction of new buildings for patient care and research, given that in my meetings with the board, several members had indicated they were not enthusiastic about an expansion. That would be a battle I would wage another day.

My final point was that I would devote a portion of my time to my own research in the lab. I needed to stay in touch with the latest scientific developments and continue to develop my drug prospect, HMBA, which I still believed could be a significant new anticancer therapy. Also, collaborating with young investigators was stimulating and helped ensure that the institution was embracing creativity and innovation.

Within a week, I received a brief letter from Rockefeller saying that he supported my aggressive vision. I went to work on July 1, 1980, with more leverage to influence all the institution's divisions than any of my predecessors.

nine

GETTING AGGRESSIVE IN THE WAR ON CANCER

TAKING ON THE JOB OF chief executive at Memorial Sloan-Kettering meant far more than a move from the West Side of Manhattan to the East Side. It was a humbling honor as well as a heavy responsibility. Columbia had felt like home—I had all but grown up and matured as a scientist at the university—and I had been comfortable managing by instinct. Now I oversaw an entire medical complex—the hospital and the research institute—and had a far larger budget at my disposal. But I had to organize and tame all these many parts to deliver better results. I intended to maintain the highest standards of science and integrity—and then push some more—because the stakes were so high.

I faced an enormous and complex challenge, confronting a disease that was still defeating us while working shoulder to shoulder with the elites from the business and scientific worlds. It was a heady experience, bringing with it some anxiety, but also a powerful sense of how far I had come in my own life from my rather modest start.

I spent my earliest years in a sheltered world with, to put it mildly, limited horizons. I was from one of the very few Jewish families in the small Pennsylvania coal-mining town of Ashland. My father, a Russian Jewish immigrant, ran a clothing store at one end of the main street. Our home, above a five-and-dime, was at the other end of the street. My maternal grandparents, who were devoutly religious Jews, operated their own clothing store a few miles away, in Mahanoy City.

I had an insular upbringing; according to family lore, when I began attending kindergarten my mother had to pry me loose from her skirts. But the emotional comforts of those first years were ripped away shortly after my fifth birthday. In a horrific accident, my mother, Sarah, tumbled down the stairs of her father's clothing store and died instantly. Worse, she had been about seven months pregnant. I went from receiving parental instruction on what my duties would be as a big brother to being a terrified child at a funeral in a family that was unraveling. My world had come apart, and it would soon get worse.

My father, Robert, sold his store in Ashland and all but disappeared from my life for five years, compounding my sense of loss. I was soon whisked away to the alien streets of Brooklyn, where my father's parents lived and where I had been born. There I was bounced between beds and couches, with aunts, uncles, and my grandparents, and struggled to make my way in this unsettling new life. My father finally returned, sometime later, with a new wife and a new child, my half brother.

Emerging from those difficult years, I slowly found my footing and started to blossom in high school. My grades were strong, and I shot up to six-foot-two. I started to take an interest in girls and developed an active social life. My first real break came when, a restless young man and eager learner, I found a mentor in the high school Honors Society. The faculty adviser was Conrad Saphier, and he quickly took me under his wing. His son, who had attended the Cornell medical school, had been killed in the South Pacific in an early World War II battle. In my nascent talents, Saphier seemed to find a second chance at realizing his broken dreams, and he became a tutor and a guide.

He planted in me the idea that not only could I go to medical school, but I should, and that the first step would be to attend a top university. Given my family's straitened circumstances, my father felt that was out of the question. But Saphier came to our home and persuaded him to at least allow me to apply. During the war, racial quotas were easing to some degree, giving young Jewish men with strong academic records a chance to enter the once restricted Ivy League club. Saphier opened a door to a world I had hardly even dreamed about.

At Saphier's urging, I took the long five-cent subway ride from Brooklyn to West 116th Street in Manhattan, to apply to Columbia College. I stumbled through my interview but somehow was accepted and received a full scholarship.

Columbia was a cabinet of wonders. I had grown up curious, but knew little of the world outside my community. Now I was studying with some of the most respected professors in the country. I took Jacques Barzun's colloquium on the great books, Mark Van Doren's class on Shakespeare, and Ernest Nagel's course on Spinoza. I studied history with Henry Steele Commager and Alan Nevins. I vividly recall a class in which Van Doren dissected the role of women in Shakespeare's plays and English society in his day. I was mesmerized by the passion of his arguments and his sophistication. In another lecture, Barzun and the famous literary critic Lionel Trilling impressed on us the relevance of Greek plays to contemporary society. In their hands, there was nothing ancient about those characters or ideas. To satisfy the physical education requirement, I even joined the football team as a tackle. I drank it all in.

One of my roommates was Joshua Lederberg, a giant intellect who would win a Nobel Prize in Medicine in 1958 for his discovery that bacteria can mate and exchange genes. We became lifelong friends, and, in 1978, I was honored when he invited me to speak at his induction as the president of Rockefeller University. Two years later, Josh spoke at my induction as president of Memorial Sloan-Kettering.

From my first days in medical school, I was driven by a sense of mission. By 1980 as I departed Columbia, the medical world had made important strides in understanding the biology of cancer, as demonstrated by a string of Nobel Prizes, but I believed that we were not doing enough to use those discoveries to develop new therapies and save lives. The apparent lack of progress in developing a "cure" for cancer, or at least better survival rates, was failing not just our patients but future patients by putting at risk the resources that President Nixon and Congress had given us.

My passion on these points did not always win me friends. When others resisted my point of view, I could be, well, fervent. At one informal gathering of researchers at Columbia, a faculty member had tried to impress us with what I believed were exaggerated data from experiments in gene expression. It seemed to me that he was on a big ego trip, so I challenged him. As the argument grew heated, I reached out, grabbing him by both arms, shaking him, and demanding he stop massaging the data—an episode reported some years later, to my embarrassment, in the *New York Times Sunday Magazine,* in a cover story about my leadership of Memorial Sloan-Kettering.

Another time, at a meeting of the president's Biomedical Research Council, I publicly berated a government scientist for arguing that we could cut polio research funding since the disease had been all but eliminated in the United States, ignoring the fact that it was still a threat in most developing countries. Benno Schmidt, who was seated next to me and clearly annoyed, declared that he would have thrown me off the panel for my caustic attitude if I had not been making some good points.

In my new position, I was more visible, more vulnerable to criticism. The world of cancer research was changing, and I had to change with it. It was clearer than ever that the cure for cancer was unlikely to be found in a flash of brilliance or as the result of a single campaign—the "moon shot" approach. There would be no miracle pill or vaccination, at least in the short or medium term. Taming the disease was going to require not one insight but hundreds, the results of breakthroughs and collaborations, some stabs in the dark, and much luck. Nevertheless, many of us on the frontier appreciated that we still needed to deliver improvements or risk seeming irrelevant.

One of my first tasks at Memorial was finding new ways to improve outcomes for cancer patients, even if incremental. We had benefited from breakthroughs in understanding the biology of the disease, if slowly, but it was becoming clear that these were unlikely to deliver the knockout blow the public had been led to expect. Our aim shifted to extending lives—known as survivorship rates—and that was going to require more teamwork among the different medical disciplines.

Following on the initiatives and changes that I had outlined in my acceptance letter, I pushed ahead quickly. I proposed making all the clinical staff full-time salaried employees, which would eliminate lucrative outside medical practices for some of the clinicians, particularly surgeons. This would mean a decrease in income for some doctors, I warned the trustees, and they might choose to leave. Disruptive as these changes might prove, I stressed that I would have to persuade the clinicians and scientists to buy into the new model to make it a success. I felt that if all members of the staff were full-time and salaried, it would be easier to ensure quality and their total commitment to the center's patients.

To assemble the elements of a successful strategy, I had to get over some nervousness with regard to the position in which I found myself. I was awed, frankly, that Laurance Rockefeller had asked me to transform Memorial Sloan-Kettering, particularly at this pivotal time. At Columbia, even as vice president of the university, I had little interaction with the trustees. But at Memorial Sloan-Kettering, I received a "visit" from Laurance Rockefeller, by phone or in person, at least once a week. These discussions proved critical in ensuring that I had the board's support, even if the changes I was proposing were not popular with many staff members.

Cancer treatment, I realized, was fundamentally a social activity, not just a scientific or purely medical exercise, and approaching it in this way would produce measurable improvements. When different specialists communicated, which, for many of them, was not the norm, hurdles could be overcome. We would later codify this approach in an innovative system called disease-management teams.

Another hurdle was that patients sometimes had to be persuaded to stick with treatments that were painful and stressful. In a surprising number of cases, some patients refused treatment, or simply gave up partway through, unable to endure the pain or side effects, even if the therapy seemed to be working. Patients often felt isolated and needed help to overcome the terror that mere mention of the C word often conjured up.

Society itself was still not very understanding or supportive of cancer sufferers in the early 1980s. There were few if any walkathons, celebrity cancer tell-alls, or posters with the smiling faces of cancer survivors. Today, we casually accept that cancer is a much-discussed topic embroidered with both fear and hope; back then, all you usually got was the fear.

This reality was driven home by the Three-Mile Island nuclear power-plant disaster in 1979. I was a member of the president's commission that assessed the causes of the disaster and how it was handled. It was an interesting but troubling experience.

A series of mechanical and human errors had caused a cooling system valve to remain open at a critical time, which led to a partial meltdown of the reactor. The government took the precaution of ordering a mandatory evacuation of pregnant women and small children, which created a brief panic about a possible release of radiation and supposed epidemic of cancer.

I was impressed by the fact that the plant was actually well constructed and that, according to the data presented to the commission, the containment vessel had remained intact and had limited the release of radiation during the catastrophe. But as we examined the plant's management, I was appalled at the poor training of the workers—few had college degrees—the slipshod systems for handling problems, and the lack of oversight at the Nuclear Regulatory Commission, which was, frankly, filled with industry hacks.

Although there have been disagreements, the data I have seen support the view that there was little risk of increased cancer rates due to radiation exposure, except of course for the workers inside the plant. The real pathology was the fear that spread due to a lack of reliable information. That fear was heightened by the fact that cancer was regarded by many people as a cruel killer, able to pounce unexpectedly. For me, Three-Mile Island drove home the reality that the public's anxieties could easily trip into hysteria and that science itself could be perceived as central to the problem rather than a path to solutions. I came away with a better appreciation of the dread people felt over cancer.

In the decade following passage of the National Cancer Act, public expectations rose because of the sums being spent on research and the occasional reports of promising therapies. That worried me and led to much introspection and questioning within the medical profession. Politicians as well as some scientists and doctors had been using rhetoric that encouraged people to expect miracles.

Typical was a comment by my predecessor at Memorial Sloan-Kettering, Lewis Thomas, who enjoyed issuing rosy pronouncements about the field he loved and saw as almost magical in its powers. Just a few years after I took over, he proclaimed in his popular book *The Youngest Science*, "I look for the end of cancer before the century is over." He had also written in a report we had worked on together about the future of biotechnology research, "Human beings have within reach the capacity to control or prevent human disease. Although this may seem an overly optimistic forecast, it is, in fact, a realistic, practical appraisal of the long-term future."

He was not alone in his optimism. In the early 1980s, we began planning construction of a new facility at Memorial Sloan-Kettering, the Rockefeller Research Laboratories. It was a mammoth task and essential to maintaining our progress. At the board meeting where we finally voted to move forward after many months of planning, Laurance

Rockefeller turned to me and asked, "What are we going to do with this facility when we cure cancer?"

I was surprised, thought for a moment about how to avoid throwing cold water on the wistful mood in the boardroom, and answered, "I think, Mr. Rockefeller, we'll still have neurodegenerative diseases to work on."

This optimism stood in contrast to what we were experiencing in the cancer field. Some researchers rightly pointed out that even with the increased funding from the government, the cancer statistics, overall, had hardly budged. In a much-read 1986 article in the *New England Journal of Medicine* entitled "Progress Against Cancer?" John C. Bailar III and Elaine M. Smith argued that, by most statistical measures, we were losing the war, and badly. Between 1962 and 1982, the rate of cancer deaths in the United States had risen from 151.0 per 100,000 populations to 188.8. The rise was due in large measure to soaring rates of lung cancer, a product, in part, of recklessly passive government policies toward smoking. Nevertheless, the data were still troubling.

When the cancer mortality rate was adjusted to reflect patterns in different age groups, it too had also gone up, to 185.1 in 1982 from 170.2 in 1962. The incidence of cancer cases, the numbers of people diagnosed with various forms of the disease, had also risen. The cancer survival rate—those surviving five years or more—had improved, one ray of light, but only slightly. Clearly, the article pointed out, more could be done in the area of prevention, the one certain way to save lives.

There were some successes. The mortality rate from all cancers had dropped for those under twenty-four, though the rate had increased dramatically for people fifty-five and older. There were improvements for some specific cancers, Bailar and Smith noted, like cervical cancer and stomach cancer. But overall, they said, the picture was "dismal."

"The main conclusion we draw is that some 35 years of intense effort focused largely on improving treatment must be judged a qualified failure," they wrote. As a result, they proposed a fundamental shift in focus, with more resources devoted to prevention rather than post-diagnosis therapies, particularly since more was being learned about cancer-causing agents in the environment and the workplace.

A year later in his article "Rethinking the War on Cancer," Bailar further stressed this idea, urging that "treatment must come to be seen as a second line of defense." He concluded, "If we take the beginning of the modern era of cancer research to be the early 1950s, we have had 35 years of unfulfilled promises."

It was harsh criticism, and I agree that prevention—especially encouraging people to quit smoking, or not to get started, and to clean up industry—can provide great, measurable improvements. That, however, is not much comfort for the millions of people fighting the disease, particularly those who developed cancer through no known reason.

But while the data he cited were correct, I felt he underestimated how far we had advanced in cracking the complex biology of cancer and how much promise that held for improving treatments. But Bailar's articles, I felt, established a standard by which my leadership would ultimately be measured. Outcomes had to get measurably better.

First, before I could tame cancer, I had a mandate to unify Memorial Hospital and the Sloan-Kettering Institute and bring them under central leadership. That was a clear challenge because they had different cultures, different specialties, and a deep sense of independence.

The resistance hit me quickly and in various, unexpected ways. First, there was the seemingly mundane but delicate question of where I was going to sit. In leaving the presidency, Lewis Thomas had arranged to step into the newly created position of chancellor, but he gave no sign that he was willing to give up the president's office suite. It was a practical imposition as well as an unsubtle symbol, I felt, of the institutional resistance I faced. I was the outsider and would not be embraced easily. I was relegated to sitting in the boardroom, a long ceremonial room with a big table and no desk or filing cabinets. I tried to make do until, after a few awkward months, Lewis agreed to move as long as he got a new office suite elsewhere. I quickly made the arrangements, but the message stuck with me.

There were more substantive issues, too. One of the first came when I was preparing my first budget and called the head of the research institute, Robert Good, to ask for his funding requests. Good, a highly regarded immunologist, was one of the first doctors to successfully perform bone marrow transplants and had been heralded on the cover of *Time* in the 1970s as a cancer-fighting pioneer. But his reputation had been damaged by his involvement in the laboratory scandal that had so concerned Laurance Rockefeller several years before.

In 1974 William Summerlin, a dermatologist on Good's research team, claimed that he had solved a serious medical problem by successfully transplanting tissue between genetically unrelated mice, preventing tissue rejection by first placing the tissue in a culture medium for four to six weeks.

It was a breakthrough that seemed to open the door to easier transplantation of human tissue. The truth was disappointing. When other scientists failed in their efforts to repeat this success, a lab assistant discovered that Summerlin had blackened the skin transplant from a genetically related white animal with a felt-tip pen. In other words, rejection remained a problem.

Good's credibility as a manager was hurt by the widely publicized episode, but he had stayed on and controlled a small fiefdom at the institute. He had, I found, his own researchers, fellows, technicians, and secretaries and kept a sizable portion of the budget and the research laboratories for his personal use. He lived in a penthouse apartment in the research building.

When I asked for his budget figures early in the fall after my arrival, Good responded that he was in California and would soon be leaving for China; he couldn't get his budget data to me, he said, before year's end. That presented a serious problem because the board had requested I submit a budget for 1981, my first full year, at its meeting in November. Stuck, I contacted Good's assistant, but he informed me that he was not at liberty to share the budget figures without Good's say, no matter what my title was.

As I thought about how to respond in the following days, Laurance Rockefeller phoned to say he had heard from Good; he had told Rockefeller that if I insisted on obtaining a copy of his budget and if I took away any of his money or space, he would resign. Rockefeller, it turned out, was not unhappy to get the ultimatum. If that was the way Good felt, Rockefeller told him, his resignation might be appropriate. Good had essentially talked himself out of his job, and he left within months. It was the first of many occasions when Rockefeller stood squarely behind me and demonstrated a shrewd ability to manage change with little if any confrontation. Rockefeller's influence and support, in fact, were among the most effective tools at my disposal. He was a surprisingly modest leader, never raising his voice or pounding the table, figuratively or literally, at least in my presence. He was a careful listener and decisive when he needed to be. He phoned me regularly, asked if I had time to talk, and would often ask detailed questions about my strategy or specific operational plans. And then he listened.

If he had objections, they did not come in the form of rejections or rebuttals but, if anything, polite suggestions. He seemed to have made the decision that he was going to support me completely, at least until he was given reason not to, and when disputes arose on the board regarding my proposals, he usually decided matters with a careful comment in my favor. He would ask for a vote, and when his hand went up, most other board members followed his lead.

I quickly began instituting the changes described in my initial proposal to help knit the parts of Memorial Sloan-Kettering together. I formulated a single budget for the entire institution for the first time, with a central budgeting process. Each department submitted and negotiated their needs with John Gunn, our chief operating officer. The new process ensured that the department heads understood that all funding and expenditures came from a single financial framework, not the hospital side or the research side, as had been the case in the past.

We created a single committee for managing appointments and promotions within both the clinical and the research staffs. The committee consisted of senior members of the hospital and the institute, so everyone could weigh in on decisions, adding a sense of unified purpose.

I created one committee to allocate laboratory space both for the scientists and for the hospital clinicians who had laboratory-based research needs. Difficult as it may be for outsiders to understand, this is one of the most contentious prizes at a research institution like Memorial Sloan-Kettering, and no scientist is too mighty to avoid the occasional mud-wrestling match over obtaining sufficient square footage. And because it is both a practical matter and a status symbol, it is a vigorous intramural sport. No one takes losing well. Establishing a single oversight committee meant there were few opportunities for playing favorites. It did not reduce the emotions or infighting, but it did create some sense that all the researchers were members of a single team with a single purpose.

I also appointed a small executive committee, made up of leaders from both sides of Memorial Sloan-Kettering, to act as a sort of brain trust. This was also a first. We met once a week for two or three hours in an informal setting. There was no set agenda. Each of us could get advice on solving knotty problems and exchange information about our various concerns. It made us rely on each other and appreciate the institution's broader needs. Personnel matters were usually at the top of our agenda. On a number of occasions, these sessions helped in identifying good recruits for important jobs. We could then fashion joint efforts to persuade the candidates to join Memorial Sloan-Kettering or in cutting through some of the difficulties in deciding to open new facilities, such as our satellite clinic in northern New Jersey.

Those steps were important, but they were just a prelude to the larger, and more controversial, reforms I turned to next. I instituted, for the first time, a performance review of most of the professional staff, reproducing in effect the tenure-review panels common at universities. In the end, about half of the research staff were replaced, which I felt strongly improved the quality of the staff and promised more innovations from researchers who were at the tops of their specialties. In addition, by requiring that all of our clinicians become full-time staff members without outside practices, the center enjoyed the complete focus of its doctors all the time. Only doctors who were completely dedicated to trying to provide the best, and improved, standards of care stayed. A new kind of "war" required new kinds of rules.

ten

A PERFECT CURE—
FOR A SINGLE CANCER PATIENT

I DID NOT HAVE THE LUXURY of focusing on just one issue as president of Memorial Sloan-Kettering, or even of focusing on one issue at a time. I was required to help plan and run important fund-raising affairs, such as the annual gala at Radio City Music Hall, hosted for several years by Frank Sinatra. I helped in recruiting key staff members. I was involved in the expansion of some facilities and planning new construction. I had to coordinate our response to emergencies, such as the time one of our surgeons operated on the wrong side of the brain of a patient with brain cancer and had to immediately recruit a surgeon from New York University capable of correcting the error. I served as a liaison to our board and the New

York business community, and I communicated regularly with senior officials in Washington at the National Cancer Institute and the National Institutes of Health. In addition, I felt a personal responsibility to stay informed on developments in the biology of cancer and new cancer treatments.

And, of course, there was my own research into hexamethylene bisacetamide, or HMBA, the possible new cancer drug I had been working on with colleagues from Columbia. It had taken a backseat to my other activities at first, but then was jolted back to life with a surprising encounter I had in early 1982 with Charles Young, a senior medical oncologist at Memorial Sloan-Kettering. He had read the articles in scientific publications that my colleagues and I had written on HMBA and was interested, he said, in the promise of a drug that appeared to stop cancer cells without killing healthy cells, too. He suggested that, based on what he had read about our progress, it was time to conduct a clinical trial of HMBA with Memorial Sloan-Kettering patients.

My initial reaction was amazement bordering on disbelief. I told Young that I was reluctant to pursue a trial because our Columbia experiments had demonstrated that HMBA was extremely effective in stopping a range of human cancer cells from growing, but only in test tubes; the drug, to our great disappointment and surprise, had failed to stop tumors from growing in mice. I wanted to be optimistic about the drug, but those initial results with mice had left me skeptical.

But as Young explained his thinking, it became clearer that one of the impediments to successful drug development in the campaign against cancer in those years was that medical centers like Columbia had been slow to test innovative prospects. Only about 3 percent of the cancer patients at Columbia who were no longer responding to standard treatments—the usual candidates for drug testing—were entered into clinical trials. By contrast, about 60 percent of similar patients were in drug trials at Memorial Sloan-Kettering, based on the proven theory that testing on mice was only moderately predictive for how drugs would work in humans.

Developing trials with new and hopefully better drugs was an integral part of the mission at Memorial Sloan-Kettering. At Columbia, in comparison, most of the oncologists were in private practice, and the truth is, drug trials produce little income relative to the extra commitment of time and monitoring. They are not moneymakers, and, of course, the success rate is generally low.

I gave Young's proposal some thought and, getting over my initial reluctance, agreed to move forward. He obtained approval from the Food and Drug Administration to begin a Phase I clinical trial. The agency agreed to permit the trial based on evidence from our earlier testing at Columbia that HMBA had not been toxic when administered to mice and had demonstrated anticancer activity against malignant cells in test tubes. Today, the FDA has more stringent rules on approving human trials, but at that time, the evidence that we were, at least, unlikely to harm the patients was enough to take the initial steps.

Young and I sifted through records and consulted with doctors and identified thirty-three candidates with different types of advanced cancers—twenty-two men and eleven women, ranging in age from twenty-one to seventy-eight. Most were no longer responding to chemotherapy or chemotherapy and radiation, and in all cases their conditions appeared to be deteriorating. Traditional treatments had simply stopped working, and, in each case, the anxious patients and their families were willing to try something new.

We calculated that in order for the patients to receive therapeutic doses of HMBA, they had to take intravenous (IV) infusion continuously for up to ten days. And so we began. In five of the thirty-three patients, the HMBA caused a dangerous drop in their platelet counts, which could have led to internal bleeding, so for them the drug had to be discontinued. For the remaining patients who tolerated the drug and showed preliminary indications of improvement, we repeated the ten-day infusions every twenty-eight days for six to eight months.

Having had little experience with trials, I found the process anxious and exciting, particularly when we began assessing the initial results some months later. Five of the patients—three with breast cancer, one with colon cancer, and a fifth, a fifty-year-old woman with a serious form of lung cancer called large-cell carcinoma—showed measurable improvement, evidenced by shrinkage of their tumors on X-rays or in physical examinations and the relief of some symptoms. Four of those patients had what turned out to be transient improvements—their tumors stopped growing for some months, or shrunk, but then resumed their deadly spread. Further treatments with the HMBA failed to improve their conditions. We documented those results in an article in the academic journal *Cancer Research* in 1988.*

In such trials, no matter how well designed and how close the monitoring, it is often difficult to understand initially why one patient responds to the drug, while others show little or no therapeutic benefits. The answers to such questions can determine whether the next step is follow-up research, further efforts to refine or adjust the chemistry of the drug, or dropping the experiments and moving on. Adding to the puzzle of evaluating the results of the HMBA trial was the fact that one of the patients, the fifty-year-old woman with lung cancer, responded differently from all the others. She had a stunning and inexplicably

---

*Charles W. Young et al., "Phase I Trial and Clinical Pharmacological Evaluation of Hexamethylene Bisacetamide Administration by Ten-Day Continuous Intravenous Infusion at Twenty-Eight-Day Intervals," Cancer Research 48, no. 24 (pt. 1) (1988): 7304–7309.

positive response. This was my first opportunity to observe firsthand what amounted to a magic bullet in action. The positive results were particularly intriguing because her condition had been dire.

By the time this patient had entered the trial, her disease had spread to both lungs and the lymph nodes in her chest. Her diagnosis of lung cancer had been confirmed by examination of a biopsy of her tumor cells. The tumors had made her breathing difficult, and she had suffered substantial weight loss. In the preceding eighteen months, she had received combinations of chemotherapy drugs, but the cancer was not responding. She was probably months from death when we began the HMBA trial.

After her first six months on HMBA, we identified no obvious improvements in her condition, but, and this was important, her disease had not progressed. That was a modestly positive sign. Because she was tolerating the doses of HMBA well, we continued to administer the drug, and we monitored her closely.

I heard little further on the case for many months. Then one morning Dr. Young called and asked that I come to the X-ray viewing room as soon as possible. He said he was "excited," something I had not heard from him before.

I rushed down to the X-ray room, where Young showed me four films on a light box, each taken roughly four months apart. He said nothing, only waited for me to see for myself what his enthusiasm was about.

A Perfect Cure—for a Single Cancer Patient

The first X-ray, on the left, was taken on the day the woman had started on HMBA, and the fourth, on the far right, was dated the previous day. The masses in the early X-rays had simply melted away. Even to my inexpert eye— I'm no radiologist—the change from the first to the last X-rays was dramatic. It was hard to believe we were looking at the same patient. The most striking changes had occurred in just the previous four months.

Young explained that some of the patient's more troubling symptoms, wheezing, weight loss, and constant fatigue, were disappearing, too. She was breathing easily, and her energy was returning. It was stunning. Doctors do not frequently exhibit much emotion in the laboratory, but Young and I clasped hands as we both looked through what seemed a window of opportunity. "You realize this could never have happened if I had not come to Memorial and you had not come to my laboratory with your 'insane' idea of doing a clinical trial with HMBA," I told him. "Before this, we could not even show that it stopped a tumor growth in a mouse!"

We had saved a life. What greater good can you do in medical science? It was, nevertheless, one out of thirty-three. We had a lot more work to do.

By chance, Memorial Sloan-Kettering's board was meeting that afternoon. It was an opportunity I did not want to pass up. I had an X-ray viewing box brought to the boardroom and arranged the four films in chronological order so the trustees might see for themselves the striking evidence of a possible wonder drug in action instead of just hearing dry statistics on patient outcomes or budgets. They were impressed, even though I had to tell them this was a partial victory.

In our report of the clinical trials with HMBA in the scientific journal *Cancer Research,* we concluded: "Although it is axiomatic that most candidate anticancer drugs will produce an occasional therapeutic response, the results in this patient suggest that all patients should be treated until a clear cut outcome is observed. We have detected no evidence of cumulative toxicity to repeated administration of HMBA: nevertheless, because our series included only one patient . . . an enlarged experience would be useful."

The patient continued to receive HMBA for the next twelve years and appeared to live a full life, clinically cancer free. Within a year of the start of the trial, we also developed a form of the drug that could be administered orally, making it far more convenient for her to continue on the HMBA. Our observations of her were halted, however, after twelve years of constant monitoring. She stopped responding to our calls, and it appeared she grew annoyed with our questions and the follow-up visits. I believe she felt she had been cured and wanted to put the experience behind her. It was hard to blame her.

News articles, picking up on the results, had appeared speculating on whether we had finally found a cure for cancer, or at least a new approach that was more targeted in killing just cancer cells. Philip Boffey, a science reporter for the *New York Times*, wrote in 1985, "Tests have begun in humans of a new anticancer drug that operates on a radically different principle than conventional cancer drugs. Instead of killing cancer cells with toxic chemicals, the standard approach, the new drug seeks to change the cancer cells so that they stop their uncontrolled proliferation and resume more normal behavior."

Boffey was aware of our success with the lung cancer patient, but he noted that it was too early to declare HMBA a success because clinical trials were ongoing and had produced uneven results. The article made clear that, overall, progress in finding effective new treatments for cancers appeared to have stalled, which was, of course, true.

We had developed a novel drug that, in effect, had brought a patient back from the dead. If we did it once, it was not unrealistic to imagine we might do it again. Nevertheless, the hurdles were high. Straightforward as the results seemed, we struggled to understand why HMBA produced this remarkable response and came up with nothing but conjectures. This was cancer. These kinds of experiences were the norm, a reality that is difficult for most of those outside the profession to appreciate. In truth, we had no clear idea how the cancer cells in the patient's particular carcinoma interacted with HMBA. The preliminary speculation was that the DMSO and HMBA caused the cancer cells to mature, transforming them into normal cells that would perform their usual functions, then die. This followed from a theory some held in the 1980s that cancer cells might be immature cells, whose "differentiation," part of the maturing process, had been arrested, allowing them to grow and divide out of control. We now understand that this theory is not correct for most cancers.

And we had to consider the evidence from Johns Hopkins University and the University of Maryland, where doctors had also conducted clinical trials with HMBA. Some patients showed temporary improvements, in similar numbers to what we had found in our trial, but none of their patients experienced a dramatic remission like our "Patient 4." But we had achieved some progress all the same. One of the major drawbacks of standard chemotherapy, even today, is that it kills both normal and cancerous cells, often causing severe nausea, vulnerability to infections, and hair loss, among other problems. One of the reasons for optimism about HMBA was that it stopped the growth of some tumors with fewer damaging side effects. If it proved selectively toxic just to the cancer cells, it would mark a major advance in the war on cancer, like introducing a precision weapon to the battlefield instead of carpet bombing.

For all the hope generated by the HMBA trials, we were never able to repeat anything close to the therapeutic effect it had on the lung cancer patient, even on other patients with the same clinical diagnosis. And despite extensive testing, we never turned up a clue as to why she, and she alone, had this remarkable response. Spontaneous remissions in lung cancer patients are extremely rare.

We speculated that this fortunate woman had a cancer with a very specific and unusual abnormality—presumably a specific genetic mutation—that made her cancer responsive to the precise chemical makeup of HMBA. But at that time, we did not possess the capability to do detailed gene sequencing, so it was never more than a guess.

One of the great achievements in the war on cancer is that, today, we routinely perform genetic analysis of tumor cells to identify the mutations as well as aberrations in how the genes express themselves. Had we found those distinguishing characteristics in Patient 4's cancer, we would have known at the least who would be most responsive to HMBA by identifying this abnormality in other patients. Instead, the drug now sits on the shelf as one of many near misses.

Science magazine recently reported on a drug trial and how the new gene-sequencing technology can be applied. A group of researchers tested a drug, everolimus, on patients with metastatic bladder cancer. In a small number of cases, it produced an enduring remission of the disease. The researchers used whole-genome sequencing to identify an unusual mutation that existed only in the cancer cells of the patients who responded well, about 8 percent of the 109 people in the trial. That research will allow doctors to determine in advance which bladder cancer patients would be good candidates for treatment with everolimus in the future, improving outcomes and sparing other patients false hopes.

We conducted a second clinical trial with HMBA in late 1986, treating patients with "liquid tumors": myelodysplastic syndrome (MDS), a precursor of leukemia, and acute myelogenous leukemia (AML), which destroys normal bone marrow and can cause death within months. As we later reported, forty-one patients with MDS or AML were given continuous infusions for ten days, which were repeated at intervals of eighteen to seventy-five days.[*] The HMBA induced a complete remission in three patients and a partial remission in six others. But the remissions lasted less than six months on average, and, once again, we did not observe anything close to the "cure" enjoyed by the earlier lung cancer patient.

The publicity on these clinical studies generated dozens of letters from cancer patients, and families and friends of patients, eager to be considered for treatment with HMBA. Regrettably, we had to explain that the trials were ongoing and the results too preliminary to justify broader use

---

[*]M. Andreeff et al., "Hexamethylene Bisacetamide in Myelodysplastic Syndrome and Acute Myelogenous Leukemia: A Phase II Clinical Trial with a Differentiation-Inducing Agent," *Blood* 80, no. 10 (1992): 2604–2609.

of the drug. The truth was that HMBA was too weak to be effective in the majority of cancers, and its bad side effect—the drop in blood platelets—created a risk of some patients bleeding to death.

I went back to my colleague from Columbia Ronald Breslow, the chemist who had synthesized HMBA, and discussed trying to find an agent with a similar chemical structure that would be more potent and less toxic. He synthesized, and I tested, more than seven hundred new compounds. Some were as much as a thousand times stronger than HMBA, but we found that the more successful they were in killing cancer cells, generally the more toxic, as we reported in a 1991 article in the scientific journal *Proceedings of the National Academy of Sciences*.

After searching for chemicals that struck a good balance between toxicity and potency, we finally decided to focus on a compound that had been number 392 on our list. That choice opened a door that would save thousands of lives, not just one. Compound 392 was suberoylanilide hydroxamic acid, known as SAHA. As we refined it into a drug and then later began trials, it would turn out to be what we had been aiming for—a clinically effective anticancer drug that received government approval, made it to the market, and is saving, or at least prolonging, the lives of some cancer patients.

eleven

CHANGING CANCER CARE FROM WITHIN

PROMISING AS OUR DRUG RESEARCH was, I had to work at the same time on institutional changes to improve outcomes. The complete answer, I knew, was not going to come in the form of a pill. The old treatment models were not working fast enough, and new scientific insights, while promising, simply were not being translated as rapidly as hoped into better therapies. We had to enlist more resources, and different types of resources, to really make significant improvements in how the patients did and how the patients felt. As I had found at Columbia-Presbyterian Hospital, clinical cancer care operated in a somewhat insular world. I decided to take a calculated gamble and replace Ted Beattie, the physician in chief overseeing Memorial Hospital. Though a superb cancer surgeon, he had allowed the hospital's clinical approach to become overly dependent on surgery as the principal method for dealing with the broad range of cancers. I felt we needed a clinical leader who could expand our programs in medical oncology and radiotherapy—that is, to provide excellence in all the areas of cancer care.

Surgery is very important and can be highly effective in cases where a tumor can be removed before it has metastasized or, at the least, before it has metastasized widely. Good candidates for surgical cures represented, however, only about a third of the patients who came to Memorial in the early 1980s.

The problem was that the emphasis on "heavy cutting" had pushed other treatments, such as chemotherapy, radiation therapy, or immunotherapy, into the background. In Beattie's view, you turned to drugs or radiation only if the doctors had been unable to control or remove the cancer with surgery. I believe he saw the use of chemotherapy drugs, immunological approaches, and radiotherapy as signs of failure, not supplementary measures to help patients live longer.

I appreciated the importance of surgery, of course, but, because I had already been working on a pioneering targeted therapy drug, I believed strongly that it was time to bring more tools to bear on what was still a relatively poor record in improving the lives of cancer patients. There had been some advances in developing chemotherapy "cock-tails," that is, treatments with mixtures of drugs designed to hit different targets in cancer cells.

This combination therapy was producing prolonged re-missions in about 80 percent of children with acute lym-phoblastic leukemia, for example, but nothing as dramatic in adults. Researchers had developed the first clinically useful biomarker test for a cancer, in this case a means of detecting prostate cancer (with the prostate-specific anti-gen, or PSA, test), often well before the patient developed symptoms. Still, we were not doing well enough clinically on those patients with proven cancers.

My mission at Memorial Sloan-Kettering was to push hard on both the research and the clinical fronts and over-come our frustrations in treating malignancies. An unstated objective was to bring cancer care and the broader world of medicine closer together. They were really two separate spheres in those days, divided, among other things, by the perplexing truth that one had effective means of curing dis-eases, while the other did not.

My first call was to William Kelley, a highly respected internist and professor of medicine at the University of Michigan. I pursued him in part because he was not an oncologist by profession. He was a respected expert in internal medicine with a sound understanding of clin-ical care as well as basic scientific research. He had the breadth we needed and did not come with the blinders that I worried some oncologists wore. But Kelley politely turned me down. It was a futile recruiting effort, but it helped me appreciate the depth of the challenge I faced in broadening the clinical care at Memorial Sloan-Kettering. It also highlighted for me the divide that had developed between mainstream medical specialties like cardiology, endocrinology, or gastroenterology, on the one hand, and oncology, on the other.

I quickly identified another great internist for the job, David Weatherall, chairman of the Department of Medicine at the University of Oxford in Britain. He was an outstanding molecular biologist who had done important research on thalassemia, the blood disease that I had studied earlier in my career. I made only slightly more headway with him. I visited him in England, where we had a good discussion about the changes I was trying to implement at Memorial Sloan-Kettering, and he accepted my offer to come to New York to see our facilities and meet some of the staff. Friendly as those meetings were, he also declined.

Unsettling as that second rejection was, it forced me to think more creatively about the best way to address the shortcomings in our approach to treating cancers. As difficult as it was to admit, I had looked to "outsiders" because I was, in a fashion, an outsider myself. Of course, I had been head of the cancer center at Columbia and was now president of the largest cancer center in the country, but I had not trained specifically as an oncologist or treated many patients with solid tumors, the most common types of cancer. I had specialized in blood diseases and so-called liquid tumors.

It sounds funny, perhaps, but I don't think I was seen as a member of "the club" of hard-core cancer experts. This came across in subtle ways. For instance, I joined and was later asked to become president of the American Society for Clinical Investigation, a body designed to honor physician-scientists who had translated laboratory research into clinical advances. I was a leader at other organizations as well as the head of various scientific periodicals and, of course, had served on several presidential cancer commissions that helped develop research strategies. However, though I had joined the American Association for Cancer Research in the 1960s, I was never invited to take on any kind of leadership role. I did not feel slighted, but it did seem symbolic.

The problem went both ways. When I arrived at Memorial Sloan-Kettering, only three of our scientific staff were members of the National Academy of Sciences, which recognizes achievement in a range of scientific fields. It was not because we did not have excellent scientists, but because, I believed, cancer specialists were not consistently on the academy's radar. (Since 1980, eighteen staff members of the center have been made members of the academy.)

The rejections from Kelley and Weatherall taught me that we were going to have to change Memorial Sloan-Kettering from within the oncology community. It would take rigorous self-examination. So my next candidate for physician in chief was Samuel Hellman, the enormously capable director of the Joint Center for Radiation Therapy at the Harvard Medical School. He was a card-carrying member of the cancer community, and he had the breadth and background to move Memorial Sloan-Kettering's radiotherapy department into the top ranks. I also thought he would be a magnet for new talent. Hellman had been highly recommended by a friend, Henry Kaplan, the head of radiotherapy at Stanford University Medical School, who said he was probably the best in his field. Kaplan was frank, however, and said he doubted I could recruit Hellman because of Memorial Sloan-Kettering's reputation for giving priority to surgery.

Because my whole aim was to change that, I went ahead anyway. When I called Hellman, I told him that, good as Harvard was, Memorial Sloan-Kettering offered a bigger platform. If you come here, I said, you will have the chance not just to run but to build something of great significance to the field. He was cordial and said only that he would give it serious thought.

I was pretty confident that I had made a convincing case, but heard nothing for weeks. I wondered if maybe silence was his answer, that he just wasn't interested, but I knew he was a man of great integrity and he would not just let an offer like this drift. I decided it meant he was really wrestling with it. About four weeks later, my wife and

I were reading in bed when the phone rang a little before midnight. "It's Sam Hellman," my wife said. I took the receiver, listened for a moment, muttered, "Great," and then hung up. "He just said, 'I'll come,'" I said. "That's it. We did it."

Hellman's decision was transformative. He came to Memorial Sloan-Kettering in mid-1983 and quickly hired other talented oncologists for key jobs. These included Zvi Fuks from Hadassah Medical Center in Israel as head of the Radiotherapy Department, which he had to build almost from scratch, and John Mendelsohn, from the University of California, San Diego, to chair the Department of Medicine (he would later take over at the MD Anderson Cancer Center in Houston, Texas). Murray Brennan came from the National Cancer Institute as head of surgery, and Richard O'Reilly, an expert in bone marrow transplantation, was made chair of pediatrics. By moving Memorial Hospital to develop its therapeutic strategies, Hellman improved patient outcomes with a range of innovative clinical programs that would influence the way cancer care was delivered across the country.

Two additional assets were the immense philanthropic contributions from remarkably generous individuals and foundations—which have risen from $33 million in my first year to more than $300 million in 2011—and the very solid support of the Society of Memorial Sloan-Kettering Cancer Center. The society, a large group of women volunteers, not only raises significant sums of money for programs but also contributes time to improving patient care and helping in the essential process of educating the public on cancer prevention and screening for early detection. They make up an important link to the community at large.

In spite of these key appointments, much of the press about my early years covered what I was removing rather than what I was adding. As promised in my initial letter to the board, I initiated two programs that thoroughly revamped the staff of the institution. Up to that time, most of the doctors had private practices and worked at Memorial Hospital part-time. It was a lucrative system for them—and was typical of most hospitals—but I felt it distracted doctors from a focused commitment to providing cutting-edge cancer care.

I instituted a system in which our clinicians had to give up these outside practices and become full-time staff members or leave the institution. For most, that meant a substantial cut in income, but there were benefits: it relieved them of the responsibility for providing nursing care, office assistants, or billing staff, and they no longer had to find and rent offices or purchase supplies. As staff members, all that was provided to them by Memorial Sloan-Kettering.

The new system attracted clinicians who were deeply committed to providing the best and most innovative cancer care. The successful implementation of the full-time, fully salaried clinical staff and the many administrative changes were to an important extent due to the skills of John Gunn, whom I had recruited as the executive vice president, our chief operating officer.

The next step was to create a more rigorous academic environment and set high-quality standards for the research staff. I instituted a tenure process, which included peer-review panels to evaluate the performance of each staff member. I recruited an overview committee of eleven members from various academic institutions, chaired by Daniel Nathans, a professor of microbiology at Johns Hopkins University, who had won a Nobel Prize in 1978 for his pathbreaking work with recombinant enzymes and their application in molecular biology. (His discoveries laid the foundation for the isolation and manipulation of genes, a critical research tool.)

The reviews were long and thorough. I brought in Joyce Stichman, who had been my administrative assistant in the dean's office at Columbia, to provide support for the review process. More than 250 staff members were assessed over three years. After all the evidence was weighed, only 90 or so were recommended for continuing appointments. Not surprisingly, that was a source of enormous controversy. A cover article in the *New York Times Sunday Magazine*, in 1987, emphasized the staff shake-up as the hallmark of my administration. "At Memorial Hospital, the center's famous clinical arm, once-powerful surgeons known for 'heavy cutting' are no longer the dominant faction," wrote the reporter,

Philip Boffey. "Marks' administration has boosted the roles of radiotherapists and doctors who treat cancer with chemical and biological agents, and has made the hospital more research-oriented. At Sloan-Kettering Institute, the center's research arm, there is increased emphasis on molecular biology, today's hot field, to balance the center's research in immunology, the glamour field of the 1970's."

But many feelings were hurt in the peer-review process, and some capable people were forced to leave, not because they lacked skill but because they were not working at what the panels believed were the highest academic standards. Boffey quoted a surgeon who had left in anger as saying, "Marks is a kind of administrative Rambo."

What the reporter did not know was the fact that, at meetings of the Board of Trustees, some influential members shared those concerns. J. McLain Stewart, a senior partner at the McKinsey & Company consulting firm, felt my aggressiveness was harming morale, creating a toxic environment.

John Reed, the future chief executive at Citicorp, questioned the whole idea of tenure. He worried that without the prospect that they might be fired for poor performance, the researchers would grow complacent. I argued that tenure had worked in academia for decades in large part because it lifted this anxiety. It allowed scientists to take more creative approaches and to pursue unpopular or novel ideas, rather than just those that seemed to offer the highest probability of producing academic papers or short-term success. They did not need to be worried that their careers would be threatened if they found themselves up a blind alley.

The atmosphere grew so heated that at one meeting, a board member directly challenged Benno Schmidt, who had succeeded Laurance Rockefeller as chairman, over the anger he felt my changes were generating on the staff. Schmidt came to my defense. "We have fewer people today than when [Marks] came, and we brought in 35 to 40 scientists and clinicians," he said. "Anytime you make that kind of change, not everybody is going to stand up and cheer. Some have to get the bad news. But Dr. Marks has no hidden agenda. What you see is what you get." With Rockefeller, now the chairman emeritus, also behind me, the talk stopped.

By that time I had come to the view that a "cure" for all cancers was very unlikely, no matter what had been said in the early days of the war. But we did have the capacity to accelerate the incremental improvements we hoped to start making in patient survival rates and, indeed, to cure at least some types of cancer, particularly in children. It would take closer collaboration between researchers and clinicians, I felt.

It also meant confronting what was becoming a perplexing moral challenge in the campaign to treat and tame cancers—was it worth focusing on treatments or new drugs that, while hopeful, might extend the lives of cancer patients by a few months at best? The research and development process for new anti-cancer drugs can run into decades, and the costs are enormous, often many tens of millions of dollars. What if, at the end of that process, we had a drug whose benefits were so modest that some patients might well decline to bother taking it?

I discussed this with my colleagues from time to time, and we usually arrived at the same difficult conclusion—it was a dilemma without a clear answer. From the societal perspective, some of this research seemed ill-considered, as those resources might be focused on research into preventing the disease or into drugs that seemed to offer a better chance of yielding cures. I often heard this line of reasoning from health care policy experts, those who sought to focus on the big picture. But I did not often hear it from the medical clinicians themselves. There was a simple reason: from the point of view of many patients and their families, the benefits of a few extra months of life can be of paramount importance. That reality did not make the dilemma go away; it just meant that we had to cope on a case-by-case basis with hard decisions about what really constituted improved treatment and improved patient outcomes. We had to focus on finding treatments that were better than what we had.

In the midst of this retooling campaign at Memorial Sloan-Kettering, we held commencement exercises on

May 26, 1981, for Sloan-Kettering Institute doctoral candidates in biological research and awarded prizes to some of our most talented students and faculty for their achievements. Robert Merton, a great pioneer in the sociology of science and a mentor to me at Columbia, was the graduation speaker and received an honorary degree. Merton was a student of the way scientists work and how laboratory findings get translated into innovative treatments. In our award citation, we noted candidly, "We have not always taken advantage of the new perceptions you have consistently unfolded relative to the scientific enterprise; we are not necessarily improved; but we surely have less excuse to prolong our follies after you have illuminated them."

I embraced that criticism as my charge in the years ahead.

twelve

ENLISTING A MAJOR NEW ALLY— THE CANCER PATIENT

I N FEBRUARY 1983, Enid Annenberg Haupt, a philan-
thropist and Memorial Sloan-Kettering board member,
called me to say that her friend Laurance Rockefeller
had suggested she consider a donation to help refurbish
our dilapidated outpatient facility. She asked if I could
arrange a tour and explain what we hoped to do. A few
weeks later, she stepped out of a yellow cab on East Six-
ty-Seventh Street, where I had been waiting. Tall, per-
fectly coiffed, wearing a beautiful suit and white gloves,
she offered her hand, and then we began to stroll through
our heavily used and outdated outpatient clinic. Haupt's
father, Moses Annenberg, had built a fortune as the publisher of the *Daily Racing Form* and the *Philadelphia Inquirer.*

Her brother, Walter Annenberg, formed Triangle Publications and founded *TV Guide* and, among other publications, *Seventeen* magazine, where Haupt served as publisher and editor. But she came to be known best for her enormous generosity. She donated her considerable fortune to everything from the New York Botanical Gardens, where the conservatory is named for her, to the National Gallery of Art and the Metropolitan Museum of Art.

We spent an hour in the crowded four-story outpatient facility. I gave her a lot of credit for her hands-on approach, and I did not sugarcoat the reality. The care the clinic provided was excellent, but the waiting rooms were jammed and the chair cushions torn and discolored. The paint was chipped.

Haupt took it all in, and then we headed back to the street. "That was more depressing than a Turkish bus station," she said. "How much money is it going to cost to rebuild this place?" I told her the architects had estimated it would take about $45 million, including space for a proposed new radiotherapy department. "I will make a gift of $25 million," she said briskly. "My lawyer will call you in the morning."

The new outpatient facility opened in September 1991, with much more than fresh paint and new chairs. It was a subtle new front in the cancer-treatment revolution, part of a shift in strategy to improve clinical care, and, not incidentally, it was part of a broader shift that contributed to changes in how the American public talked and thought about cancer. By bringing many patients out of the hospitals, we were helping bring cancer out of the shadows and making cancer treatment facilities more appealing, more supportive, and less impersonal. The new facility had a Radiation Oncology Center, a Surgical Day Hospital, and office suites for the doctors. Haupt's taste and generosity even extended to underwriting the cost of daily fresh flowers. The new facility had other important innovations. Put simply, we had determined that the more our patients spent time at home with their families, and the less time in the hospital, the better the outcomes. The issue was not just comfort but better health. The patients stayed healthier psychologically and, in many cases, embraced their treatment regimens with a greater degree of commitment. And not incidentally, the cost of care dropped as patients spent less time in the hospital, which was often unnecessary.

The challenges of cancer go well beyond its lethal tenacity and mutability. One striking but common factor is that some patients simply give up after being diagnosed and refuse to stick with all aspects of their treatment. At times, patients abandon treatment that can be harsh and painful. I have seen this happen many times, even with friends who sought my advice after being diagnosed with cancer and whom I had encouraged to stick it out. The onset of this alien disease is too much to bear for many patients, so making the treatment regimen less intimidating and ensuring that patients stay close to their family support systems can produce more effective therapies.

Those concerns shaped a number of initiatives that began to alter popular perceptions of cancer treatment. My colleagues at Memorial Sloan-Kettering and I realized that there was a great deal that we could do to enhance the lives and prognoses of patients beyond trying to conjure up cures in the laboratory.

My determination to move Memorial Sloan-Kettering in this new direction came partly from Patricia Mazzola, chairman of the Department of Nursing. In 1981 she and some of her colleagues had come to see me to discuss the possibility of establishing an adult day hospital. Her reasoning was straightforward: patients who had diagnostic procedures or chemotherapy were routinely held in the hospital for stays of a day or two at the time, but, she explained, almost 80 percent were well enough to be treated at a day facility and then return home in the evening. The physical and psychological comforts of home went a long way toward reducing the often debilitating stress and anxiety of cancer treatment. This could improve the quality of patient care and reduce costs considerably. Mazzola estimated that 80 percent to 90 percent of patients receiving chemotherapy, some of whom stayed for up to three days at a time, would make good candidates for a day hospital.

At the time, providing this level of care in a day hospital for cancer patients was a novel approach and required the approval of the New York State Department of Health. It was not easy. An adult day hospital for cancer patients was considered a major departure from standard protocol in most instances, and the burden fell on us to demonstrate that patients would not be harmed.

The state was reluctant to license us unless we could prove in a controlled study, spanning several years, that the day-hospital patients would enjoy outcomes at least comparable to those who were treated as in-patients. We persuaded the state to grant us operating status as "an experimental program," so that we could undertake a three-year study, a time period we considered appropriate to develop sound conclusions and establish that the patients did as well or better than those receiving in-patient care; in fact, they felt they had a better experience, we determined, and it came at roughly one-third less cost.

The Adult Day Hospital, the first of its kind for providing intensive outpatient cancer care, became a model for many other cancer centers across the country. The national significance was enormous because cancer was then the number-one cause of hospitalization in the United States. By 1990 we also opened the Surgical Day Hospital, which offered patients, when appropriate, "same-day" surgery— such as breast or lymph-node biopsy or removal of localized skin cancers—in a calm and attractive setting.

Those successes made us rethink many aspects of how we delivered clinical care and the elements that made up successful treatment. Patients could receive treatments for as long as twelve hours in a comfortable hospital room and then return home. Over the next two decades, Memorial Sloan-Kettering built more than a dozen outpatient care facilities in the New York tristate area. That represented a sharp departure from the previous centralized approach of providing all care at the main Memorial Hospital.

In 1985 about 30 percent to 35 percent of our patient-care revenue came from outpatient services; by 2003 the figure was 50 percent, and it reached almost 65 percent in 2010. Total outpatient visits have risen from 141,000 in 1980 to 536,000 in 2011.

Not all the clinical improvements involved bricks and mortar. Other initiatives introduced fresh approaches that improved the quality of life for patients and also made them more committed to their treatment programs. Patients' lives and comfort, rather than just their malignancies, became the focus of care.

We took another step in 1982 when Kathleen Foley, a neurologist on our staff and a dedicated leader in cancer-pain research and care, introduced a pioneering pain-treatment service for cancer patients. Recognizing how horrible the pain associated with the illness and treatments can be, she created the first systematic, focused program to relieve this challenging symptom of the illness. She had conducted studies showing that about one-third of cancer patients in active therapy experience pain and two-thirds of those with advanced disease experience significant pain.

Foley and her colleagues developed novel and more effective pain-relief methods—for instance, a drug related to morphine that was more potent with fewer withdrawal problems. To implement her ideas, she established a nurse fellowship program and, for doctors, two-year clinical and research pain fellowships. Aggressive efforts to alleviate pain became integrated into cancer treatment plans rather than being an afterthought.

Another significant innovation was introduced by one of our psychiatrists, Jimmie Holland. A cancer diagnosis, especially in the mid-1980s, when survivorship rates were much lower, caused great psychological distress. Surgery and other treatments can also create anxieties about body image, among other things. Even cancer survivors can develop chronic anxiety and depression as they contend with the possibility of recurrences, which are common with many forms of the disease. But neither Memorial Sloan-Kettering nor any other cancer center had programs specifically designed to understand and treat this distress. The hospital's attitude had largely been "They've been treated; we have nothing further to offer." Holland made the psychological well-being of patients, not just their bodies, an essential ingredient in the treatment model by creating the field that came to be known as psycho-oncology.

Holland persuaded me of the importance of her approach, but I also benefited from prodding by my wife, Joan, who was trained in psychiatric social work and also believed that addressing emotional stresses helped patients confront the challenges of cancer treatments. We instituted a practice, partly at her urging, that every patient was seen by a social worker who would ask questions about anxieties and fears and offer patients the opportunity to see a member of the psychiatry staff.

That was a ray of light in a somewhat dark world. Patients and families coped with the disease alone, treatments were harsh, and the prognoses, more often than not, were bleak. Holland took another big step by focusing on the emotional health of cancer survivors. The stigma of a cancer diagnosis made it difficult for them to discuss their fears and concerns about life after treatment, and they received little institutional support. In her research, Holland had found that the most common effects of coping with death and dying were anger, fear, anxiety, depression, financial worries, and family stress. At some point, about 50 percent of cancer patients suffer emotional symptoms severe enough to be diagnosed with a psychiatric disorder; about 25 percent of those patients suffer from much more acute clinical problems that can interfere with the cancer therapies and usually require intensive treatment and medications—a very large number. Holland became the first chair of Memorial Sloan-Kettering's Department of Psychiatry and Behavioral Sciences, the first department of its kind in a cancer center. She went on to become the founding president of the International Psycho-Oncology Society and the American Psychosocial and Behavioral Oncology Society, ensuring that other cancer centers learned about and adopted mental health programs.

Holland would tell cancer patients, "You are the real experts and teachers because you know what it is like to cope with these questions. Ask questions and tell your doctor what you feel. Do not be timid or reluctant to speak out."

Nevertheless, embracing her ideas was not a smooth process. Some of our cancer surgeons and medical oncologists frankly regarded her focus as peripheral to their treatment regimens and even somehow less "scientific" than surgery, radiation, or drugs. Some surgeons approached me privately and demanded to know, "Why are we doing this?" These psychiatrists are not treating the cancer itself with any accepted drugs or therapies, they insisted. They felt the new department called into question the fundamental scientific character of the institution.

In short, they believed that any department not devoted squarely to killing cancer cells was a waste of resources—and a dangerous flirtation with therapeutic mumbo jumbo. These naysayers were misguided and shortsighted. Over time, Memorial Sloan-Kettering and other prominent cancer centers accepted Holland's contributions, and patients have undoubtedly benefited.

Another first for a cancer center was the genetics counseling program, established in the late 1980s. About 5 percent to 10 percent of cancers are associated with hereditary vulnerabilities to the disease. This program counsels patients who are at risk—based on family history or detection of a genetic marker, such as the BRCA gene, which predisposes women to breast cancer. The program, headed by Kenneth Offit, is an important component of Memorial Sloan-Kettering Cancer Center's prevention and early-detection services.

We also started to chip away at the walls separating some medical disciplines. Under the previous model, a patient was diagnosed by one group of doctors and then passed to another set for interpreting the results and formulating treatment options. The surgeons might step in to remove a tumor and then hand the patient over to medical oncologists or radiotherapists. In addition, each specialty was physically separate, leaving it up to the patients to navigate the maze of buildings and hallways.

I sat on the board of directors of the Pfizer pharmaceutical company at that time, and one day a discussion about a new marketing idea prompted me to think about how we could break down our barriers at Memorial Sloan-Kettering. One of Pfizer's executives discussed a marketing plan for a diabetes drug. A complex, chronic illness, diabetes requires management of many aspects of the patient's lifestyle, including diet and exercise, monitoring of blood-sugar levels, and medication. Pfizer wanted to provide physicians with brochures describing an entire diabetes management system as a way of stimulating demand for Pfizer's new drug.

I realized that cancer, too, could be treated more effectively if the diagnostic and therapeutic programs were coordinated in this manner. This may sound obvious today, but it represented a big change at that time, when each part of the process was separate and relatively autonomous. We created multidisciplinary teams, each of which coordinated the care of patients. Those teams communicated more closely while coordinating the testing, monitoring, and treatment. Each type of cancer has its own team. One of the trickiest aspects of implementing this innovation turned out to be developing computer software that would allow each member of a team to track, sort, and analyze the diagnostic and treatment information from all the locations where the patient was seen. This included everything from appointment schedules to X-rays, biopsy results, and medications.

I described this challenge to another Pfizer board member, John Opel, who was a good friend and the chief executive of IBM. Opel saw this as a potential business opportunity for the computer giant and arranged for a team from Memorial Sloan-Kettering to meet with IBM experts at their research center in Poughkeepsie, New York.

In March 1984 I joined the team, which included clinicians, nurses, researchers, and our executive administrator,

John Gunn; the physician in chief, Sam Hellman; and Dick Rifkind, head of the Sloan-Kettering Institute. Over three days, we addressed the full range of requirements for the system that would support the disease-management teams.

Several weeks later, the head of IBM research delivered the surprising news that the volume of the inputs was so great and diverse that their software designers did not believe any single system had the capacity to track patients as we wished. The problem was technologically far more complex, he said, than landing a man on the moon.

The news was sobering. I discussed the problem with the chairman of the board of Memorial Hospital, James Robinson III, then chief executive of American Express. He recommended that we speak with a company called Cambridge Technology Partners, made up of a group of MIT professors.

After a thirty-day study of the hospital's systems and requirements, they suggested breaking the information down into smaller segments rather than trying to tackle everything at once. It took Cambridge Technology three years to develop the software, but they finally delivered a digital treatment and management system.

The system enhanced patient care, reduced errors, decreased adverse drug reactions, and gave doctors more timely information and access to the latest "best practices" for more than ninety different types of cancer. In addition to tracking all the patient treatment information, it calculated expected costs, which made it easier to control them. Memorial Sloan-Kettering became the first health care provider in New York State to effectively go paperless, a model for other hospitals and cancer centers.

One of the more unusual new patient-care initiatives grew out of one of my many weekly conversations with Laurance Rockefeller. At times my secretary would buzz to alert me that Mr. Rockefeller was on his way just as he opened the door of my office. He often began conversations about details of our operations or strategy in the middle of a thought and just carried on. He concluded these informal explorations by saying, "This has been a wonderful visit!" whether we had spoken in person or by telephone, and he was usually right.

In the early 1990s, Rockefeller invited me to his office for a luncheon meeting that was a little more philosophical than usual. It was in Rockefeller Center in a suite of offices for family members. After I greeted him, he walked me across the hall to the office that his older brother Nelson had once occupied. Nelson had died in January 1979, but Laurance told me that everything had been left precisely as it was on that day, even the paperwork on the desk. We sat at a little round table in Nelson's office and were served Laurance's favorite lunch—consommé, saltine crackers, and cheese sandwiches on white bread.

Laurance had a strong spiritual streak, though not always in a traditional sense, and he occasionally told me that he believed healing required that we attend to the souls of our patients, not just their bodies, and consider employing nontraditional methods. Now, he said, that was what he had invited me over to discuss. "I want to endow a program that will provide a holistic approach to the care of each patient," he said. "Memorial should have a program of complementary care that addresses the spiritual and emotional as well as physical needs of patients."

I am a man of science, and he knew I had reservations about the value of alternative approaches like massage therapy, music or art therapy, or meditation for treating a disease as medically challenging as cancer. And so he made me an extremely shrewd offer. He said that he not only proposed to endow a new program in nontraditional types of healing, called integrative medicine, but would also provide funding for better "translational research," which would come under my direct leadership. That program would speed up the process of translating laboratory discoveries on the biology of cancer into new clinical treatments or therapies, something he knew I was keenly interested in developing.

Rockefeller donated $10 million in 1998 to establish this dual program, and he sought to overcome the skepticism among the hard-nosed surgeons and oncologists about alternative therapies by emphasizing that the overall aim was to bring new approaches to the "bedside." That was something, like motherhood, that few could oppose, and it guaranteed that Memorial Sloan-Kettering would fulfill his vision and offer, to those who were interested, a holistic approach to cancer care.

Later that year, Rockefeller wrote to me, "I remain enormously grateful to you for your personal involvement and commitment to this effort. What is particularly gratifying to me is that we have become co-venturers in this process and have joined in a shared vision for Memorial's future success."

We were able to persuade an established expert in this field, Dr. Barrie Cassileth, to come out of retirement and become the first incumbent of the Laurance S. Rockefeller Chair of Integrative Medicine. She had more than twenty-five years of experience and had published extensively in the field. She had developed research programs on topics like the effect of botanicals on the immune system and the role of various complementary medical interventions in cancer care.

Memorial Sloan-Kettering's integrative medicine program now offers touch therapy, mind-body therapy, acupuncture, creative therapy, reiki massage, and nutrition counseling, as well as exercise programs to improve strength and promote relaxation. The services are available to anyone receiving cancer care at Memorial Sloan-Kettering or elsewhere and to the general public as a whole.

When patients who are interested in these methods have access to them, we have found, they often comply with their medical treatment regimens better and are less likely to turn to what I regard as quackery, drugs or dubious herbal treatments that, in many instances, do not work and can be harmful, especially if they pull the patients away from proven medical therapies.

These innovations and patient-focused programs in cancer care did not "cure" cancer, of course, but they removed some of the unnerving mystery of the disease and improved the quality of life of many patients. In doing so, they made all of us appreciate that better outcomes could be influenced by more than better anticancer drugs or other medical treatments. It was another step in the long-term process of removing some of the very heavy burden of living with cancer. It was also a prelude to the introduction of one of the biggest symbols of the improving understanding of the disease and of the efforts to transform it into a chronic but treatable illness—a small pink ribbon.

thirteen

BREAST CANCER
GETS ITS OWN HOME

T HE TWO WOMEN SITTING in adjacent seats in the surgical waiting room of our outpatient pavilion looked fine, other than the conspicuously anxious looks on their faces. They were surrounded by an array of young and old patients bearing the signs of serious cancers: oxygen tanks, IV tubes, heads stripped of hair by chemotherapy, pale and taut skin, emaciated limbs. The two women looked as though they had wandered into the wrong building. This was not an uncommon scene for the waiting rooms of the outpatient clinics in the mid-1980s, but when I noticed these women, I began to wonder if perhaps they were in the wrong place.

I had a tendency to think of progress in cancer treatment mostly as the solving of a series of scientific conundrums by molecular biologists, but observing those apparently healthy women made me more conscious of the vital human dimension of our job at Memorial Sloan-Kettering. More likely than not, both women had discovered a lump that indicated they might have breast cancer and had been referred to us for diagnosis and treatment. We saw it all the time. But they were, as is often the case with early-stage breast cancer patients, outwardly healthy. They were just starting to contend with the prospect of an illness that, while quite serious, we were getting better at treating.

Their lives might not have been seriously disrupted yet, and they might not ever be. Yet here they were, confronting the worst effects of the disease in the waiting room. It was depressing and demoralizing, and I began to wonder if something could be done to ease the entry of such patients into the challenging world of cancer care.

From that initial impulse, I consulted with colleagues, and we developed the novel idea of building a separate clinic just for women with breast cancer. No one had done anything like it before.

Because breast cancer patients are different in some ways from others, we thought the treatment should reflect that. For one, it obviously affects women and only rarely men. It is also a disease of a part of the body that, for many women, is intrinsically bound up with their sense of identity and femininity. Our society sees a woman's breasts as elements of beauty and sexuality, and, of course, they have a fundamental connection with the distinctly female role as mothers. Why not, we asked, develop a facility that reflected these distinctions and provided more sensitive comprehensive care?

We began to envision a center that would provide the most up-to-date breast cancer prevention, diagnosis, and outpatient treatment services as well as a wide range of support services, all under one roof. It would have its own special disease-management team, including oncologists, radiotherapists, pathologists, genetic counselors, psychiatrists, and social workers, and offer a comprehensive set of services, save for surgery, which required the operating-room facilities of the main hospital. Our board offered its energetic support.

Despite the fact that no one had heard of a free-standing breast cancer center, a number of doctors—including Sam Hellman, the physician in chief of the hospital; Larry Norton, the head of the breast cancer unit; and all the breast cancer staff—seemed enthusiastic about the idea. We hired experts to design a facility that was, in a sense, more emotionally supportive and, perhaps, more feminine and soothing for patients and families. That left two issues to resolve, raising money for the center—we thought it would require about $20 million—and where we would put it.

I discussed the plans with our board chairman, James Robinson III. He suggested I work with his wife, Linda Robinson, a highly experienced public relations executive, to conjure up ideas for the funding. She suggested that for funding, we should approach the industry that sells beauty and femininity—cosmetics. She reasoned that contributing to women's health would be another way for the companies to connect with their clientele and give something back.

We visited some large cosmetic firms, including Revlon, L'Oreal, and Estée Lauder, but the attitude was, "We cannot sell cosmetics and cancer!" Mixing beauty and disease was too much of a downer. It was a discouraging start for what we hoped would prove an important innovation in women's health care, a subject that, though common today, was just starting to be discussed in the 1980s and was being helped along by a few notable cases of prominent women speaking out about their experiences with cancer.

When First Lady Betty Ford disclosed in 1974 that she had breast cancer and had had a mastectomy, it was one of the first instances of a highly visible woman publicly discussing her diagnosis. It was a brave admission, and it raised awareness and the comfort level for public discussions of cancer. In addition, Happy Rockefeller, Nelson Rockefeller's wife, disclosed she had had breast cancer shortly after Betty Ford. We needed to continue the effort.

By chance, another public figure's breast cancer contributed to the improving attitudes, and in this case I was personally involved. In October 1987, I was startled one day in the office when my assistant told me, "The White House is on the phone." It was the first lady, Nancy Reagan. She explained that she had been diagnosed with breast cancer and faced some difficult decisions about treatment. She asked if I could advise her—over lunch, the next day, at the White House.

I rushed to Washington, and she explained her situation. Her doctors had found a tumor, and she was presented with two options. The first, the least invasive, was to have a lumpectomy—relatively minor surgery to remove just the cancerous tissue—followed by a course of chemotherapy with the possible addition of radiotherapy. Those treatments would likely force her to withdraw from public events for some time because of the side effects, including possible hair loss. She was very reluctant to do that because several important state visits were scheduled, including one by the Soviet leader, Mikhail Gorbachev. Her second option was a mastectomy, a more extensive and serious operation. It would require some time to recover, but it would probably not require further therapy and so would put Mrs. Reagan out of action for a shorter period of time.

She wanted to opt for the second option, she explained, but felt uncertain about the ultimate impact on her health. I advised her that if she had two options that her doctors regarded as equally effective and would leave her healthy, the choice was entirely hers.

She proceeded with the mastectomy and not only recovered well from the surgery, but also discussed her cancer in a television interview and encouraged women to have regular mammograms. She undoubtedly helped increase public understanding and public comfort with the subject.

Mrs. Reagan was delighted when in a later conversation I told her that her publicity appeared to be encouraging more women to get breast cancer screening. That was not the last I would hear from her. Some months later, to my surprise, she invited my wife and me to a state dinner. I had been to plenty of formal galas for Memorial Sloan-Kettering and other prominent institutions, but this was an extraordinary experience. After our car brought us to the front of the White House, each of us was walked to the entrance by the waiting marine escorts amid an array of well-known politicians and celebrities. We were star gazers in that crowd and were amused to hear some of the photographers whispering to each other, "Who are they?"

It was a pleasant step on the path toward better treatment for breast cancer patients, but our initial efforts to obtain funding for Memorial Sloan-Kettering's new center were falling far short of the goal until 1989. This time I got an unexpected call at home one evening from Leonard Lauder, the head of the Estée Lauder cosmetics company. He was calling with the unfortunate news that his wife, Evelyn, had been diagnosed with breast cancer, and they were hoping she could be treated at Memorial Sloan-Kettering.

I made the arrangements for her care. Evelyn Lauder was a senior corporate vice president at Estée Lauder and a superb marketer, and I later had the chance to discuss with her our plans for a freestanding center dedicated to breast cancer, from prevention and early detection to diagnosis, therapy, and survivorship programs.

She got what we were trying to accomplish right away and offered to help. In short order, she threw herself into the planning, connecting her name and the family's company with the cause, and was instrumental in raising the nearly $20 million we needed. It turned out that cosmetics and cancer care were not as antithetical as others had supposed.

As we pushed ahead with the planning for the breast cancer center, we quickly realized that we did not have room for the breast cancer center within the Memorial Sloan-Kettering campus, so once we moved into the design phase, we had to find new space. Our representatives approached several East Side building owners about leasing space, but the landlords refused to rent to us. They felt that having cancer facilities in their commercial buildings would be just too frightening or uncomfortable for many people; it might scare off tenants, or customers.

It reminded me a little of the days when doctors were worried about treating cancer patients for fear the disease was contagious—in the eighteenth century. The Lauders came to our aid again and found suitable space at East

Sixty-Fourth Street between Second and Third Avenues. The landlord insisted that we not put up a prominent sign at the front of the building for the breast center, but he relented on renting to us because the location had been originally intended for a garage, so it was out of the way, or, rather, hidden.

Evelyn Lauder held a press conference on the site to announce the project, and former president Gerald Ford, whose wife, Betty Ford, had been so instrumental to the cause of breast cancer awareness more than a decade earlier, was the main speaker.

Mrs. Lauder was deeply involved in the center's design and planning. It included a shop for prosthetics and wigs for women who had lost their breasts from mastectomies or their hair to chemotherapy. As a talented nature photographer, she contributed many handsome photographs and other art that was hung throughout the center.

The innovative clinic, named for Evelyn Lauder to commemorate her energy and generosity, opened in 1992. It was the first of its kind and a trendsetter for the world of cancer care. It has since been replicated around the United States and in other countries. The center has not just led to better treatment, but also brought a new level of awareness and public engagement with cancer. The stigma was lifting, though it would be a long process.

The war on cancer had not produced the miraculous "cure" that many had wished for, or had been led to expect, but we had achieved hard-won incremental improvements in treatment outcomes. Patients were not only starting, little by little, to live longer, in at least some cases, but also enjoying a better quality of life. And those fighting the disease did not have to hide or be afraid to speak out, as though they were afflicted with something shameful.

Evelyn Lauder threw herself into another step in this process by founding, with Alexandra Penney, then the editor of *Self* magazine, the pink-ribbon campaign and the Breast Cancer Research Foundation. It quickly turned into a marketing cyclone and put music into the lives of many depressed cancer patients.

Anyone who has recently witnessed the spectacle of the giant athletes of the National Football League sporting pink shoes, pink towels, and other pink accessories during the annual Breast Cancer Awareness month every October understands how successful the campaign has been in nurturing an image of cancer as a disease that can be managed, if not always beaten, and that can be discussed. The program, in addition to raising hundreds of millions of dollars to augment research and training, educates women about prevention, genetic testing, early detection, and treatment methods.

Memorial Sloan-Kettering subsequently opened a new Evelyn H. and Leonard Lauder Breast Center in October 2009, as part of a sixteen-story breast and imaging center, financed by a $50 million gift from the Leonard and Evelyn

Lauder Foundation. It is a long way from the East Side garage where our idea first took root.

By then we were making significant progress in applying our research discoveries on the genetics and biology of breast cancer to more effective treatments, making the Lauder Center much more than a handsome, comfortable clinic. The five-year survival rate for women had risen to more than 90 percent in the mid-2000s from about 60 percent in the mid-1950s.

Progress in analyzing the gene and molecular tissue of each patient's breast cancer is reshaping our understanding of the disease and leading to novel and effective treatments. We have discovered multiple subtypes of breast cancer, each presenting different cellular targets that we can try to hit with cocktails of drugs.

The expertise that the new breast center brings to the problem has made it possible to provide an individualized treatment strategy—surgery and, if indicated, radiation and drug therapy—that targets the specific type of breast cancer and the specific genetic defects in the tumors. The model of a dedicated facility is also being applied to other forms of cancer at Memorial Sloan-Kettering, including prostate cancer, colon cancer, melanoma, and gynecological cancers.

fourteen

LEARNING TO LOVE ACID

FTER THE PROMISING, if mixed, results of the
clinical trial of HMBA in 1988 discussed earlier, I
continued my research at Memorial Sloan-Kettering
with a group of postdoctoral students.

In those clinical trials with HMBA, not long after I had
arrived at Memorial Sloan-Kettering, I had watched in as-
tonishment as over a period of months, one of the patients,
the fifty-year-old woman with advanced lung cancer, had
enjoyed an almost miraculous response to the drug. She
had a 50 percent reduction in the size of her tumors after
receiving HMBA for eight months, and she survived for
at least twelve more years. We do not know exactly how
much longer she survived because we lost touch with her.

Even though most of the patients in the trial had at best
temporary remissions, we believed that fundamentally the

drug had enough promise that we should try to refine the chemistry of the compound and produce a better version that was more potent and less toxic. That is when we began to explore the new chemical, number 392 on our list, suberoylanilide hydroxamic acid. It was called SAHA.

Our painstaking efforts helped open up a new area of cancer research and drug development, known as targeted therapy. Instead of killing both cancer cells and healthy cells with powerful toxins, the carpet-bombing approach, we conducted a focused counterinsurgency against cancer's devious acts of cellular sabotage—by targeting only the offending abnormal cells.

We hypothesized that some part of the HMBA molecules was engaging in a well-known process called "binding," in which the drug and a part of a molecule within the cancer cell are pulled together. Some portion of the chain of atoms that make up the drug has an almost magnetic-like attraction to part of a molecule within the cancer cells.

Many anticancer drugs work by binding tightly to and then blocking the actions of the target molecules in the cancer cell that drive its irregular growth; the stronger this binding action, the more potent the drug. We believed that the acid portion of the HMBA acted as the binding agent to the cancer cells, and so we tried to develop a new drug that had a similar acid molecule in its structure but would prove more potent.

SAHA had the same type of acid in its structure, and it turned out to be one hundred times more powerful than HMBA in killing or arresting the growth of cancer cells in test tubes. That was a good start. Next, we gave it to mice in which we had transplanted a human prostate cancer. SAHA completely inhibited the tumor growth at doses that had little or no toxic effect on the mice.* We then gave SAHA, orally and by injection, to mice with five other types of cancer and had similar results: growth of the tumors was stopped with little apparent toxicity.

Though pleased with these initial results, the truth was we still understood next to nothing about exactly why SAHA was so effective; what was the engine of its success in stopping the runaway growth of the cancer cells? To construct more potent versions of the drug that we could use on human cancer patients, we had to understand this process at the molecular level. It was exciting and frustrating.

The big clue in unraveling how SAHA worked came serendipitously during one of the regular weekly meetings I held with the researchers in my lab. It was 1996. Victoria Richon, who had joined my laboratory at Memorial Sloan-Kettering in 1986 as a postdoctoral fellow and then become an assistant professor, listened to a presentation by one of the postdoctoral fellows on an article by three

---

*Lisa M. Butler et al., "Suberoylanilide Hydroxamic Acid, an Inhibitor of Histone Deacetylase, Suppresses the Growth of Prostate Cancer Cells in Vitro and in Vivo," Cancer Research 60, no. 18 (2000): 5165–5170.

Japanese researchers about a chemical, called Trichstatin A, or TSA. The Japanese had discovered that TSA had a similar effect on mouse leukemia cells as the chemical that started our exploration, DMSO; it switched on the process of producing hemoglobin, turning the cells red, while stopping the cancer-cell growth.

The "Aha!" moment came with the article's description of TSA's chemical structure: it was, Richon noted, similar to SAHA.* Further, the researchers found that TSA inhibited the function of an enzyme called histone deacetylase, or HDAC. As the Japanese wrote in one of their articles, "These results clearly indicate that TSA is a potent and specific inhibitor of the histone deacetylase and that the in vivo effect of TSA on cell proliferation and differentiation can be attributed to the inhibition of the enzyme." It was a complex description, but it led to a straightforward, and exciting, question: had we found our target?

The Japanese researchers had found that TSA—a chemical, produced by a bacteria, that is sometimes used as an antifungal agent—caused an accumulation of what are known as acetylated histones. In simpler terms, acetylation is a chemical process in which a small chemical group, acetyl, is bonded to a large protein molecule (R), in this case

$$\left[\ R - O - \overset{\overset{\textstyle O}{\|}}{C} - CH_3\ \right]$$

---

*M. Yoshida et al., "Potent and Specific Inhibition of Mammalian Histone Deacetylase Both *in Vivo* and *in Vitro* by Trichostatin A," *Journal of Biological Chemistry* 265, no. 28 (1990): 17174–17179.

histone. That process alters the structure and function of histone and other proteins that are involved in regulating the way that genes express their coded instructions. It also affects proteins that regulate cell growth, migration, and death. In other words, HDACs were important to the function of cancer cells, sort of microscopic chemical accomplices, helping them survive, as well as in the life cycles of normal cells.

We went to work and were quickly able to reproduce the experimental results reported by the Japanese researchers. Now, though, we substituted SAHA for TSA, and eventually we found that SAHA also blocked the action of a specific group of HDAC enzymes.

In cancer cells, the enzyme was acting as a catalyst, triggering an unhealthy chemical reaction that caused the cells to grow out of control. SAHA was able to prevent this unhealthy process from taking place.

This significant breakthrough was the result of what the Nobel laureate François Jacob, one of my mentors at the Pasteur Institute, called "night science," a scientific exploration that relies on intuition as much as it does on the cold, orderly pursuit he described as "day science." It led the way to a better understanding of how an abnormally functioning enzyme, not just a gene mutation, a strand of defective DNA, could be involved as a root cause of cancer.

There are eleven different HDAC enzymes that are widely distributed throughout human cells. Each one has a different role in the biology of cells, and each has a metal ion, zinc, embedded in its structure that is critical to its activity. We discovered that SAHA was a potent inhibitor of several of these enzymes. The HDACs inhibited by SAHA play a role in the regulation of cell proliferation, cell death, cell migration, and metastasis. In normal cells, the HDACs ensure that cells develop properly, perform their functions, and then die. In cancers the switches on those control mechanisms somehow get reversed, allowing the cells with abnormal HDACs to grow out of control.

Abnormal HDAC enzymes are found in many cancers. They can be the result of mutations in the HDAC gene that created them, or they can result from errors in the chemical process that takes the coded information from the gene and uses it to produce HDACs. Either way, abnormal HDACs can transform normal cells into deadly cancer cells.

Inhibiting or blocking the abnormal HDAC enzymes with SAHA effectively turns the switches back to "normal," causing cancer cells to stop growing and to die. Most of the chemotherapy drugs used for cancer are, in effect, poisons that kill both healthy cells and cancerous cells. The trick is to use doses that destroy as many of the malignant cells as possible without killing too many normal cells or causing serious damage to the patient's health.

SAHA is different. It does not kill cells indiscriminately. It is much more surgical in its strikes. It blocks the HDACs in both cancerous and healthy cells, but the healthy cells, we found, are able to quickly (within hours) recover from the impact, while the cancer cells cannot recover. Instead, they die. That is why SAHA, we learned, produces few side effects. It is a targeted therapy.

In 1999, working with my colleagues at Memorial Sloan-Kettering, we gained further information about how SAHA works. Using X-ray crystallography, we were able to take what amounts to a snapshot of an HDAC as it interacted with SAHA at the molecular level. These images revealed to us that the part of the enzyme that is responsible for its activity—the catalytic site—had a zinc atom embedded in its structure. The hydroxamic acid in the SAHA molecules latched onto that zinc atom.

The SAHA molecule is shaped almost like a long snake, and the zinc atoms in the HDAC enzymes sit at the bottom of a pocket that forms its catalytic site. The long, narrow SAHA molecule reaches down into that pocket so that the hydroxamic acid end of the chain can bind tightly with the zinc.*

This seemingly technical observation had profound importance. Most scientists had believed that to turn a defective gene off or on, you had to somehow change the structure of the DNA itself. This is, for example, how cancer-inducing viruses turn healthy cells into malignancies.

---

*Michael S. Finnin et al., "Structures of a Histone Deacetylase Homologue Bound to the TSA and SAHA Inhibitors," *Nature* 401, no. 6749 (1999): 188–193.

But our studies, reinforced by similar work being done by researchers at several other laboratories, showed something different. Alterations in the structure of critical proteins that are attached to genes—rather than altering the structure of the DNA of the genes themselves—could alter the way genes expressed their functions, and that, in turn, could alter how cells behaved. This important insight came to be known as "epigenetic" control of gene expression.

Epigenetic therapy is now a rapidly growing and very promising area of anticancer drug research. In fact, it appears it may be a useful approach in treating other disorders as well, such as neurodegenerative diseases, autoimmune disorders, AIDS, and metabolic diseases.

Epigenetic therapy has spawned a new medical industry. In 2001 the scientific publication *Nature Reviews Cancer* invited me to write its first overview of the current research on HDAC inhibitors. That required reading, and summarizing the findings, of almost four hundred scientific publications. Just eight years later, in 2009, I was asked to update the review; my search of the literature revealed that close to nine thousand papers on the subject had been published just in the previous twelve months. (With that discovery, I declined to write the updated review.)

Once we found that SAHA stopped the growth of a number of cancers in mice and had few toxic side effects, we decided that it was time to initiate human trials. We applied to the Food and Drug Administration for a Phase I clinical trial, which is designed primarily to determine the toxicity of the drug on humans and may also provide evidence of its effectiveness. The FDA approved our application in January 2000. It was twenty-five years since my colleagues and I had started down the path of developing a new type of anticancer drug and about a decade since the HMBA trials had concluded.

Seventy-three patients with advanced cancers, ranging from mesothelioma and non-Hodgkin's lymphoma to prostate and thyroid cancers, were chosen for treatment. Of those, five patients had a greater than 50 percent reduction in their tumors, and, just as we had seen in the previously discussed trials with HMBA, one patient had a complete, almost miraculous remission.[*]

That remission was particularly heartening because the patient was a nineteen-year-old girl with large B-cell lymphoma who had exhausted all other treatment options and appeared to be near death. When she started on SAHA, she was bedridden and had been forced to drop out of college. Within months of our treatment, her symptoms disappeared. I had seen this happen to the lung cancer patient during the HMBA trial, but it is remarkable to observe the phenomenon in progress and uplifting to see a young person regain hope. She suffered some side effects from

---

[*]William Kevin Kelly et al., "Phase I Study of an Oral Histone Deacetylase Inhibitor, Suberoylanilide Hydroxamic Acid, in Patients with Advanced Cancer," *Journal of Clinical Oncology* 23, no. 17 (2005): 3923–3931.

SAHA like nausea and diarrhea, but she returned to school and her health was restored for the seventeen months she received the drug. As hard as it had always been for me to experience losing patients with whom I was associated in one way or another, even though I was not personally treating patients on a regular basis, my occasional sense of failure was replaced in this instance by a new sense of purpose. The story, however, did not end there.

Different doctors take different treatment approaches, and, even in the best of times, clinical decisions can be a mix of science and art. Factors such as the patient's state of mind and the difficult side effects from drugs can play a role in determining strategies.

The young woman's physician, an oncologist in private practice, thought her response was so positive that she could stop taking SAHA. I pleaded with him to reconsider and keep her on the drug, fearing that a cessation could allow the lymphoma to return. He and the patient decided, however, that she was cured.

Sadly, her cancer returned within weeks. We tried restarting the SAHA treatments, but her cancer did not respond this time. Presumably, the cancer had mutated in a way that made it resistant to our therapy, a common occurrence. SAHA may have killed one type of cancer but not the new, mutated version. The patient, that bright young woman, soon passed away. It was a heartbreaking way to learn the lesson that SAHA could be extremely effective, but as long as the patient was responding, it had to be administered continuously. Later tests showed that even when there were remissions from SAHA, they were at times temporary and the disease returned after many months, or even years. What stood out with this young woman was the depth of her recovery on the drug and the absence of symptoms.

Nevertheless, we had made enough progress to expand the clinical trials. We wanted to use SAHA on different types of cancer and at other cancer centers to determine if we had a drug that was ready for the market. But setting up broader trials would be quite expensive, and Memorial Sloan-Kettering was not, understandably, willing to cover the costs, given the uncertainties we still faced in producing a viable anticancer drug for the market. We approached several large pharmaceutical and some smaller biotechnology companies to see if they would be willing to finance the trials in return for the prospect of licensing a successful drug later, but they were reluctant. Their chemists said they believed that a polar compound like SAHA was potentially too toxic to make a good drug for humans. Even though the results from our trial proved otherwise, we simply could not persuade them the drug was safe. In a meeting with the top scientists at one big-pharma company, one of their senior officials questioned our data and flatly insisted that we were mistaken about the claimed therapeutic benefits of a polar compound; I was outraged, and we got up and walked out of the room.

We then decided to take an alternative approach. We established our own biotechnology start-up, which we then used as a vehicle to solicit financing from venture capital companies. The risk was high, but the reward could be significant if SAHA proved effective, and venture capital companies were generally more willing to bear such risks than the big pharmaceutical companies. (The rewards for success would be shared by our institutions, as Columbia University and Memorial Sloan-Kettering owned the patent on the drug and received licensing fees.) Health Care Ventures, a Boston-based venture capital firm, agreed to invest in our firm, "Aton Pharma," which we formed in 2001. Aton was the ancient Egyptian sun god who shone down on the populace: an appropriate name, given our high hopes.

As planned, we used our new financing to get started on some additional trials in several cancer centers. Madeleine Duvic, a dermatological oncologist at MD Anderson in Houston, Texas, led a trial focused on patients with cutaneous T-cell lymphoma (CTCL), a rare cancer for which there was no effective treatment. Their response to SAHA was impressive; more than 60 percent of the patients enjoyed some relief, and about one-third of the patients had a significant regression in their tumors.

The success of this clinical trial finally attracted the attention of a number of pharmaceutical companies. The prospect of their acquiring a successful drug was now higher and the risks of outright failure much lower. So in 2004, Merck acquired Aton to continue the testing and prepare SAHA for the market. With its substantially greater financial resources, Merck was able to complete additional clinical trials, and in October 2006 the Food and Drug Administration approved it as a treatment for CTCL patients. It was given the generic name vorinostat. Meanwhile, trials are continuing to determine if SAHA is effective on other types of malignancies.

Today, there are hundreds of programs in big pharmaceutical companies and biotechnology companies, as well as academic institutions and the National Cancer Institute, to develop other types of HDAC inhibitors to treat almost every major type of cancer.

fifteen

THE PAYOFF

I N 1980, THE YEAR I ARRIVED at Memorial Sloan-Kettering, a total of 184 out of every 100,000 Americans died from cancers. That was second only to the perennial number one, heart disease, which took 336 lives out of every 100,000. But even after a decade of change at all the major cancer centers and the transformation of Memorial Sloan-Kettering—installing an outstanding staff, adding numerous patient-care innovations, starting new drug trials, and creating novel programs for easing the crushing pain of cancer and ministering to the darker anxieties of patients—the mortality data had barely changed. In fact, the national statistics had worsened. A total of 215 out of every 100,000 Americans died from cancer in 1992. Heart disease mortality rates, however, had improved, dropping to 290 deaths out of every 100,000.

Mortality rates are a blunt instrument for measuring success in the cancer war, and they can be misleading. It can take years, for instance, if not decades, for the "insult" that triggers the disease to create a cancer diagnosis and longer still for a malignancy to kill. The figures also reflected the fact that incessantly rising lung cancer rates, a product in part of years of aggressive, unimpeded cigarette marketing, were a key factor in pushing up the brutal cancer death figures. We were making great progress in treating some forms of the disease, such as childhood cancers, as well as breast and prostate cancer, but they could not keep up with the toll from tobacco use. In the end, though, the death rates do tell you something important about the medical field's ability to treat serious cancers, and in this case the message was not the one we wanted to hear.

I was president of a single cancer center, so I was not in a position to control the battle nationwide, but Memorial Sloan-Kettering was the largest cancer center in the United States, a trendsetter whose practices and innovations influenced the entire field. We struggled to deliver great science and great treatment, but the real test, ultimately, was saving and lengthening lives. Were we succeeding? During the 1980s and early 1990s, our qualified response to that question was not yet, but we were getting closer.

What we could say for sure was that our understanding of cancer biology and how it turns our own cells against us had grown exponentially in a relatively brief period. Today, it is easy to lose sight of how rapidly our knowledge of the disease grew from next to nothing to great sophistication. The 1980s saw the beginning of the second of the two great intellectual pivots around which the cancer campaign turned. The first was the revolution in molecular biology and genetics, accelerated by Watson and Crick's discovery of the double-helix structure of DNA only thirty years earlier. Molecular biology allowed us to understand the mechanisms by which cells grow, divide, and die and eventually gave us the tools to examine, manipulate, and explain the intricate chemical engines driving the machinery of life.

It is generally not appreciated how recently we developed this deep understanding of the gears and pulleys of the cell, in part because, unlike space or deep-sea expeditions, the exploration of our inner space has not taken place on television or offered a comparable visual spectacle. Many know that Neil Armstrong was the first man to skip across the surface of the moon, but how many know who discovered the oncogene, the genetic triggers that can cause cancer?

Lewis Thomas described this scientific epoch in his 1974 book, *The Lives of a Cell*. He called the stunning advances in cell biology "a curious, peaceful sort of revolution that, remarkably, won us over not by overthrowing an old order, like, say, the Copernican revolution in astronomy, so much as inventing a new regime previously unimagined."

"Whole, great new blocks of information are being brought in almost daily and put precisely down in what were previously empty spaces," Thomas wrote. "The news about DNA and the genetic code did not displace an earlier dogma; there was nothing much there to be moved aside."

By fathoming, finally, how normal cells conduct their business, we developed insights into how cancerous mutations subvert healthy cells and their metabolic pathways, transforming them into devious killers. Knowing which molecular switches they throw when hijacking the machinery of life, we were devising strategies for stopping cancers.

As Nobel laureate David Baltimore had said, those laboratory successes made the earliest years of the war on cancer "heroic times," scientifically speaking, when many profound questions about normal and abnormal cellular behavior were illuminated. That probably would have happened with or without Nixon's increases in spending on research, but surely more slowly. It might not have happened, however, had the early debate on the focus of the war on cancer placed the highest priority on a frantic search for "cures" over fundamental scientific knowledge.

But those insights took us only partway toward formulating therapies for stopping malignancies. One of the crucial problems with cancer is that the defective cells use myriad tools to succeed in their relentless assaults; it is not like, say, smallpox, which spreads and kills in one way. There are many ways cancers get started, a profusion of ways they turn healthy cell division and growth into lethal attacks, and many means by which these shape-shifters outsmart the body's normal defenses. Also, cancer cells and their abnormal genes are inherently unstable, so when a barrier is put in their way in the form of a drug, they can often mutate around it, over and over, fighting off anything that gets in their way.

Developing these insights represented one of history's great scientific leaps, all the more impressive because they were accomplished over just a few decades. When I had led my medical school class's "cutting-edge" honors seminar on cancer in 1949, we had only a vague understanding of the composition of DNA, were not certain where it was located, and had no image of its architecture.

When I began to study the pathways of metabolism in cells as an ambitious young researcher, I had to map them almost from scratch, starting with the relative simplicity of a spinach leaf. When my Columbia colleagues and I first observed in the 1970s the way the solvent DMSO had tripped a molecular switch in mouse leukemia cells, allowing them to produce hemoglobin, we had not really understood previously that those kind of cellular signals could be manipulated that way.

The second historical pivot took shape in the 1980s and 1990s, as researchers started to weave these biological insights into more coherent patterns. We finally came to know the story of cancer as a kind of scientific narrative with plot twists. We were shedding light on how cancer puts its vicious stratagems into practice and conducts warfare against our organs. And that allowed us to formulate new methods for interrupting or stopping these assaults.

We had learned how the genes in healthy cells mutate—at times, pieces of DNA break off and are reshuffled; at others, there is a subtle realignment of the nucleic acids, the building blocks of DNA. These mutations can give off signals for hyperactive cellular growth, overexpressing the normal growth message. Those abnormal genes are the so-called oncogenes.

Michael Bishop and Harold Varmus, working at the University of California in San Francisco (Varmus would later succeed me as president at Memorial Sloan-Kettering), laid the groundwork for understanding oncogenes. Scientists had also found that another set of genes operates in tandem. In healthy cells, they regulate and stop cell growth when appropriate. They are "suppressor genes," and they, too, play an essential role in the story of cancer. Cancerous cells find ways to prevent the suppressor genes, sort of cellular police, from doing their job.

Once those key cellular actors were identified, we began to understand how in many cancers the oncogenes are stimulated to race out of control and the suppressor genes are silenced, in a shrewdly coordinated assault on the software of the healthy cell. Reversing that previously unknown switching process became the focus of research. Adding to our understanding was research by Bert Vogelstein at Johns Hopkins University. He identified a specific suppressor gene, a protein called p53, which works by sniffing out damaged DNA. It stops cell division until the broken DNA is repaired, preventing the propagation of cells that could potentially cause cancer. These discoveries amazed us with the intricacy and beauty of our cells' natural capability to suppress cancer-causing mutations. But on some occasions, cancers disable these healthy preventive checkpoints, allowing abnormal cells, wolves in sheep's clothing, to slip through.

Vogelstein also described the process by which abnormal cells in the colon can develop into polyps and then get transformed into malignant tumors. Judah Folkman of Harvard discovered the signals that tumors send out to support their growth by stimulating the development of blood vessels to feed their voracious appetite for nutrients. He called this angiogenesis. The insight opened the way to development of a new class of drugs, called anti-angiogenesis agents, which work by inhibiting the expansion of the blood supply to tumors.

The first such drug using this insight was Avastin, or bevacizumab, a monoclonal antibody. It blocks a protein called vascular endothelial growth factor (VEGF), which triggers growth of the new blood vessels. Blocking the VEGF can, in theory, starve tumors and halt their growth. There are now a number of innovative drugs being developed that try to prevent expansion of blood-supply networks.

After years of painstaking work in the lab, researchers found that a lethal but rare cancer, chronic myelogenous leukemia, was triggered initially by the breakup of two genes. Two pieces of these genes, they discovered, recombined into a new fused gene that controls production of tyrosine kinase, an enzyme involved in the production of white blood cells. In the CML cells, the enzymes produced by this new fused gene, instead of engaging in the regulated activity of normal enzymes, spur the runaway manufacture of white blood cells, which can be life threatening.

These insights, which took several decades to come together, subsequently led to formulation of a drug, Gleevec, a chemical smart bomb that disarms the faulty tyrosine kinase enzymes. The result is lifesaving reductions in white blood cell production. Gleevec treatment of CML was one of the early successes in developing effective, targeted anticancer drugs. More have followed.

Researchers enjoyed a similar success with the development of Herceptin, another targeted lifesaver. Herceptin is a monoclonal antibody that stalls the growth of breast cancer by impeding the functioning of a defective gene, called the Her-2 receptor. About 35 percent of women with breast cancer have this genetic defect in their tumors and generally respond to the drug.

In addition, brilliant lab work demonstrating how viruses can cause some human cancers opened the door to other new treatments. In a few instances, viruses infect human cells and create mutations that can turn normal cells malignant. Human papillomavirus can cause cervical cancer, the Epstein-Barr virus can trigger various lymphomas and carcinomas, and hepatitis infections can lead to liver cancer. These discoveries have led to development of vaccines that prevent some malignancies.

Advances in radiotherapy are also delivering more effective treatments and improved outcomes. Pulses of radiation have been used for decades to shrink tumors and kill cancer cells, but in the new era, the technology was rethought, refined, and reinvigorated in ways that produced better results. Staff at Memorial Sloan-Kettering helped develop three-dimensional conformal radiation therapy and intensity-modulated radiation therapy. These computer-guided methods deliver beams of energy from many angles, with greater accuracy and higher intensity, minimizing damage to the surrounding healthy tissue while maximizing the impact on tumors.

Though significant, those advances have not immediately extended or saved the lives of cancer patients in the numbers we have been hoping for, and that has been a source of tension. Some critics, including some doctors, have complained that, decades after war was declared in Washington, our efforts are not just failing, but misguided; too much money, they argue, has been devoted to basic research on issues that interest scientists but have little direct bearing on saving lives. I believe that, although I share their frustrations, some of these critics do not understand the complexity of cancer and its biology.

In cancer biology, like every other scientific field, plenty of time is spent on dead ends and unproductive ideas in part because we do not know in advance which leads will generate practical breakthroughs. Also, some researchers may not understand the full implications of their work, or how it might be used to open up new areas of exploration. They write an article, planting an idea, and see if that seed takes root and grows.

Consider how my colleagues and I developed the targeted therapy SAHA. The Japanese scientists who discovered that an antifungal agent caused mouse leukemia cells to begin producing hemoglobin saw the observation as little more than a footnote to their scientific enterprise until the researchers in my lab spotted its potential usefulness in the development of SAHA.

Some critics argue that far too much time and money are spent on the development of drugs or other treatments that extend lives by a few months at best. How, they ask, does society benefit from this apparent misapplication of resources when the results are so underwhelming? Why bother lifting the expectations of sick patients who would get so little out of the treatments?

It is a fair question. On many occasions, I have discussed and debated the issue with colleagues. As researchers, we move into the development process with the hope that a new drug will add significantly to the life span of cancer patients. No one knows in advance that the benefits might provide just a short reprieve before the cancer takes its lethal course.

What I have found is that, in most instances, the patients themselves, and their families, do not question the benefits. They might express anger and frustration. They might question the cost of some expensive treatments, or the quality of life of the patient, but not the fact that they have a few more precious months with a loved one. I was struck recently by a touching personal essay in the *New York Times* by the author Joan Marans Dim on the long, painful death of her husband from cancer. In the piece, headlined "A Decade of Goodbye," she reflects on the difficulties she and her husband confronted as he wasted away and finally succumbed to the disease, and she wonders if a quick death might have been better. "We were married 52 years," she concludes. "What reasonable person could ask for more? And yet, if I had one wish, I'd add just five more minutes."

The more practical and thoughtful criticisms, in my view, have focused on whether the medical community has done enough to agitate for prevention, which is a better way, in some respects, to reduce mortality rates. It is a fair point. Effective treatments for cancer have been and perhaps always will be devilishly hard to conjure, be slow to develop, and potentially have a limited shelf life because of cancer's evasiveness. So it does make sense to work harder to help people avoid the disease in the first place. To some extent, we know how to do that.

The easiest preventive step would be to stop people from smoking cigarettes. They are the greatest self-inflicted wounds to our nation's health. Tobacco causes more cancer deaths than any other single factor, an avoidable tragedy. According to the American Cancer Society, 443,000 Americans die prematurely due to smoking a year from various illnesses, of which 49,400 die from secondhand smoke. Smoking causes about 30 percent to 40 percent of all cancer in the United States.

Although the government has declined to ban cigarettes, it has taken aggressive measures to discourage smoking, including high taxes and minimum age limits on purchases and startling health warnings on packs and in ads. A growing number of restrictions have also been placed on where people can smoke, making the habit ever more inconvenient and antisocial.

New York City, which has instituted among the most restrictive laws in the country, offers clear proof that the tough measures against public smoking work; there is no doubt that cancer rates will improve as a consequence. The overall smoking rate in New York has dropped from 22 percent in 2002 to about 14 percent. What is particularly heartening is the even more dramatic decline in youth smoking; according to the city's health authorities, the smoking rate in the city's public schools has tumbled from 18 percent in

2001 to 7 percent in 2010. By contrast, the youth smoking rate nationwide declined from 29 percent in 2001 to 20 percent in 2009. The cigarette century, with its catastrophically tragic costs, is hopefully drawing to a close.

We have known for years that industrial workplaces produce many cancer-causing chemicals and that even sunlight and radiation can produce malignancies. Italian physician Bernardino Ramazzini wrote in the late seventeenth and early eighteenth centuries that some occupations, principally mining, appeared to induce cancers and other diseases in workers. In the eighteenth century, an English physician, Sir Percivall Pott, attributed the high incidence of scrotal cancer among chimney sweeps to prolonged exposure to coal soot.

Given that long history, and research into more contemporary carcinogens, the issue in prevention is not knowledge so much as the will to limit or prevent exposure. These are questions for politicians and government policy makers. Many offending agents, including asbestos, coal tars, and certain fungal toxins such as aflatoxin, have been reduced, producing fewer incidences of mesotheliomas, cancer of the lining of the lungs, and forms of leukemia. The question is not whether preventive measures would be effective—we know cancer rates would fall—but the cost: whether the public could be persuaded to give up certain habits and, perhaps most important, where the funding for prevention programs would come from.

Such measures would save countless lives. It would, however, be a grievous error if they were funded by cutting back on research into better cancer treatments. No matter how many cancers are prevented, there will still be many tens of thousands of people diagnosed with cancer every year. They deserve the best possible care and the promise of improved therapies, which can come only from continued investments in basic science and new drug development.

Those investments were being made and, by the end of 1990s, proving their benefits. From a rate of 184 out of every 100,000 Americans dying from cancer in 1980, the figure had declined to 164 in 1997. The five-year survival rate for all cancer patients had increased from 51 percent in the 1974–1976 period to 64 percent in the 1995–2000 period. That was, however, just a down payment on the payoff from the research spending we were to achieve over the next decade.

sixteen

CANCER SCREENING AS A WAY OF LIFE

I N THE BATTLE AGAINST CANCER, here is a critical fact that is too often overlooked: fewer American women now get mammograms for early detection of breast cancer than a decade ago. In fact, fewer women are getting Pap smears that can identify cervical cancer, and young American women receive the three-part vaccination for the human papillomavirus, which causes cervical cancer, at a far lower rate than women in countries like Canada, the United Kingdom, and Australia.

Screening for cancers or precancerous lesions is essential for effective protection. We can sometimes spot and remove lesions before they turn into cancers, thus saving lives and money. But even when cancers have developed, if they are caught early, the chances of a complete recovery for the patient are significantly better than after the cancer has spread.

But the trends are going in the wrong direction. The number of men and women over fifty years old getting colonoscopies to look for precancerous polyps or cancers has been rising slowly, but it is still well below desired levels to protect the elderly population from this common disease, which takes more than fifty thousand lives a year. Worse, because of the cost of the procedure, the affluent get routine colonoscopies far more frequently than lower-income Americans, creating a stark class health division.

Lives are being lost unnecessarily due to cost, or complacency, or a lack of awareness of the benefits of early cancer detection. For reasons that we do not completely understand, many people seem to regard exhortations to get lifesaving cancer tests like being nagged to floss their teeth regularly. Perhaps the tests seem like an inconvenience that can be put off for another day. That is a shortsighted error that affects not just individuals and families, but society.

The National Cancer Institute reported that, in 2010, just 66 percent of women aged forty and older—those who are told they should undergo regular screening—had had a mammogram within the previous two years, down from 70 percent in 2003. Women who have no health insurance are getting mammograms at less than half that rate, the American Cancer Society has reported, which means that low-income and unemployed women are more vulnerable to breast cancer.

In 2010, according to the National Cancer Institute, only 74 percent of women aged eighteen and older had had a Pap test for cervical cancer within the past three years, down from 81 percent in 2000. Here, too, there is a serious socioeconomic divide; only about 60 percent of women with eleven or fewer years of education had had a Pap smear, according to a breakdown by the American Cancer Society, and just 56 percent of women who had no health insurance had this critical test.

In 2010 only 62 percent of people fifty and older had ever had a colorectal endoscopy. That represented a significant jump from 39 percent in 2000, but, according to the NCI, just 49 percent of Hispanics and 58 percent of blacks had had this screening test for colon cancer. These data tell an important story.

In the mid-1980s, physicians at Memorial Sloan-Kettering began a study on the importance of colon cancer screening by organizing a free screening program at our Strang Clinic, directed by Dr. Sidney Winawer, chief of gastroenterology. We screened twenty thousand patients a year, all of whom received a comprehensive health exam, too. We followed as many as possible for at least a decade. The statistics provided clear evidence that removing polyps not only reduced the incidence of colon cancer, but also helped move private insurers and Medicare to cover the cost of the colonoscopies because they reduced expenses in the long run.

The data for the HPV vaccine, which can prevent cervical cancer, is even more discouraging. In 2010 only about 50 percent of girls thirteen through seventeen years old, the prime target group, had received at least one dose of the HPV vaccine, according to the NCI, and only about 30 percent had received the recommended full complement of three doses. That is disappointingly short of the government's goal of getting the three-dose vaccination rate to 80 percent by 2020.

Memorial Sloan-Kettering recommends that women begin annual screening for cervical cancer with Pap smears at age eighteen and get regular mammograms starting at age forty. From age fifty on, people should have a colonoscopy or a "virtual" colonoscopy with a CT scanner every four to five years. Men should begin having annual rectal examinations for prostate cancer and PSA blood tests starting at age fifty. There is some disagreement in the medical community on the details of when men and women should commence screening and how frequently the tests should be administered. Different studies show different results and suggest constant monitoring is necessary and that tweaking the recommendations is a good thing. But there is no doubt that better screening tests and more frequent screening would reduce cancers significantly and advance the campaign far more quickly than waiting for the next wonder drug

We should initiate intensive new efforts to increase the rates at which Americans get screened for common cancers. Just as important, we need to finance and accelerate research into improved screening methods, as well as vaccinations for viral infections that can lead to cancer, such as the hepatitis virus. These measures would provide the swiftest improvements in cancer health outcomes since the "war" on the disease began in 1971.

If skillfully organized, better screening methods and utilization rates could reduce cancer deaths much more quickly than new treatments—which can take decades to develop—and at far less cost in suffering and in dollars. Our entire society would benefit from, among other things, the resulting decline in health care costs and increases in worker productivity.

Some efforts to increase screening have fallen short of expectations. For instance, a Center for Disease Control effort called the National Breast and Cervical Cancer Early Detection Program specifically targets low-income, uninsured, and underinsured women. In operation since the 1990s, it provides the tests for free or at very little cost to the patients.

Nevertheless, according to research cited by the American Cancer Society, the program reached just 14 percent of women eligible for breast cancer screening in the 2007–2010 period and less than 9 percent of women eligible for the cervical cancer test, in part because of inadequate funding.

Clearly, the program has to be given more funding and marketed more aggressively to come anywhere near its potential.

Research spending should also be increased to develop better screening methods that are more accurate, less costly, and easier to administer. We also have to come up with tests for early detection of more types of cancer. In terms of research dollars provided by the government, this should not be regarded as an either-or trade-off. The scientific work being done on fundamental cancer biology and on the development of new drugs to fight the disease must continue. But larger sums have to go to the neglected stepchild of cancer care, screening and early diagnosis. It is an investment that would generate enormous returns.

The government's budget priorities are resulting in a misallocation of resources. For fiscal year 2012, the National Cancer Institute requested a total budget of $5.2 billion. Of that, $3.4 billion, or more than 65 percent, was for research into the basic causes and mechanisms of cancer and the development of treatments. But support for research into early detection and diagnosis of cancer was just $455 million, less than 9 percent, while prevention research made up a mere 4.5 percent of the total, $232 million. The priorities are wrong and should be adjusted through an overall increase in spending.

In February 2011, the President's Cancer Panel concluded, "Areas that are currently inadequately addressed include cancer prevention and early detection. A shift in strategy is needed to identify informative markers for early detection of cancer; the current approach of analyzing late-stage tumors is unlikely to yield promising leads."

It is also important to understand that improvements in screening methods and technologies would not require Nobel Prize–caliber scientific discoveries. We already have good methods in hand for a number of common cancers and are working on new techniques that could be rolled out quickly, such as the "virtual colonoscopy," which can be done with a CT (computed tomography) scanner and is less invasive than the standard colonoscopy.

A great weakness appears to be in education and public awareness and funding of free programs for low-income people and the uninsured. We know that such campaigns work because a number of other countries have produced much better records on cancer screening. What is needed is the kind of clever marketing that has made the pink-ribbon campaign for breast cancer awareness such a success.

The Affordable Care Act, President Obama's health reform legislation, requires coverage of preventive services like mammograms and Pap smears with no copayment required of patients. The government reported that in the first full year the law was in effect, 54 million Americans with private health insurance had access to these screenings without having to pay. Most colonoscopies are now covered under private insurance plans and under Medicare.

A number of new screening methods are being developed that could provide even better detection. These include new imaging techniques to detect breast cancer, lung cancer, and colon cancer and some tests that may help provide early signs of other cancers.

A National Cancer Institute–sponsored study provided some important good news. The study indicated that a screening technique of the lungs using low-dose computed tomography, or CT, can detect tumors early enough to produce a 20 percent reduction in lung cancer deaths among current smokers and former heavy smokers. This marks the first time that a screening test has been found to reduce mortality from lung cancer, one of the deadliest forms of the disease. The test is a harbinger of what we can expect if screening research is funded better and made a higher priority.

One potentially powerful new technique would provide a means of finding even tiny numbers of cancer cells circulating in the blood system. We now have technology that can detect one cancer cell out of a million or more blood cells from only a small blood sample. These circulating cancer cells can be isolated and then analyzed to determine in which organ they originated, giving oncologists a very early warning of a growing tumor.

Another promising early diagnostic test being developed is the use of gene analysis of DNA fragments that circulate in the bloodstream. Such tests can identify mutations in the fragments, effectively transforming a blood sample into a liquid biopsy.

What is particularly helpful is that detection of these circulating cancer cells can be made sometimes before there is any clinical evidence of a malignancy in the patient. The hope is that once the technology is refined and the cost reduced, these screenings will be as routine as annual blood tests for cholesterol, blood counts, and other basic health indicators.

I am astounded by the richness and creativity of the research on cancer over the past half century, but I am also humbled by the complexities of the disease. Not only are we finding dozens, if not hundreds, of different genetic mutations in tumors, but there are different kinds of cancer cells with different abnormalities in the tumor of any one patient.

As my colleagues and I found with the young lymphoma patient during our first SAHA trial, cancers can develop a resistance to even the best therapies and come roaring back, deadlier than ever, after a period of remission. That is why I am not sure that we will "cure" many cancers, particularly advanced malignancies, but I am certain we can do more to catch the disease earlier in most people, when it is most easily defeated. The facts supporting this approach are compelling.

The treatment breakthroughs we have achieved have proven most effective in destroying cancer cells and reducing or eliminating tumors before the malignancies have metastasized. Once cancers have spread, they find more ways to evade chemotherapy cocktails and produce lethal effects.

Cancers have usually been identified based on the organ in which they originate and, at times, by the genetic and molecular defects found in the tumor. The diagnosis also includes a determination of the degree of seriousness, based on the size of the tumor and whether it has spread into the lymph system or other organs. This is known as the staging system, and, though it is different for different types of cancer, it is based on the idea that cancers generally progress in a similar manner as they invade organs, getting more lethal and harder to stop as they grow in size and reach. Stage I is a cancer where the tumor is small and is localized in the site where it is believed to have started. These tumors, usually two centimeters or less in diameter, are the most easily removed through surgery. Stage II cancers are generally larger, up to five centimeters, have invaded deeper into the original location, and, although they have not spread to other organs, appear to be approaching that step. In Stage III cancer, the malignant cells have spread into the lymph nodes, making it harder to remove them. Stage IV is the most advanced stage of the disease. The cancer has metastasized to other organs. It usually requires the heaviest doses of chemotherapy as well as radiation treatments.

Put simply, Stage I cancers are the easiest to control and possibly to cure; we have more tools, and the tools are more effective. Stage IV cancers are the most resistant to therapies.

Thus, success rates in treating specific cancers vary widely depending on the stage at which they are caught. According to data from the National Cancer Data Base, when breast cancer is detected and treated at Stage I, at least 95 percent of the patients survive five years or more. (The National Cancer Data Base includes comprehensive information from more than fourteen hundred accredited cancer programs.) That was in a survey of the disease from 2003 to 2008. The five-year survival rate drops to 90 percent for Stage II, 65 percent for Stage III, and 20 percent for Stage IV. That is why doctors push so hard for women to get regular mammograms.

For colon cancer, five-year survival rates vary from 78 percent for Stage I to 9 percent for Stage IV. Lung cancer, the number-one cancer killer, has five-year rates of 48 percent when treatment begins at Stage I and 4 percent at Stage IV.

Breast Cancer Survival

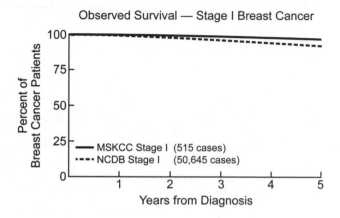

Observed Survival — Stage I Breast Cancer

MSKCC Stage I (515 cases)
NCDB Stage I (50,645 cases)

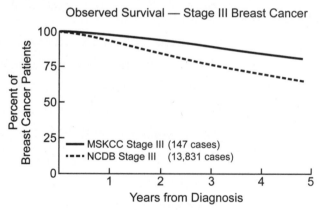

Observed Survival — Stage III Breast Cancer

MSKCC Stage III (147 cases)
NCDB Stage III (13,831 cases)

Source: National Cancer Database (NCDB), a collaboration between
the American College of Surgeons and the American Cancer Society

Memorial Sloan-Kettering has achieved more survivors
in key cancer categories, offering a model for improved
treatments and outcomes nationwide.

Colorectal Cancer Survival

Observed Survival — Stage I Colon and Rectal Cancer

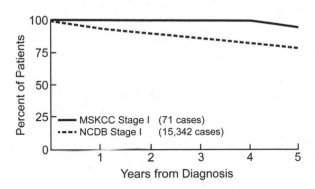

Observed Survival — Stage III Colon and Rectal Cancer

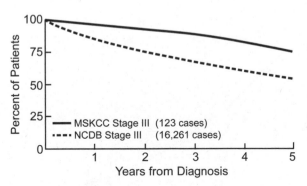

Source: National Cancer Database (NCDB), a collaboration between the American College of Surgeons and the American Cancer Society

If more adults and their primary care physicians made screening a routine procedure, more cancers would be detected at Stage I, and tens of thousands of lives would be saved every year.

Lung Cancer Survival

Observed Survival — Stage I Lung Cancer

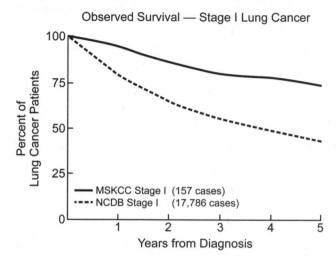

Observed Survival — Stage III Lung Cancer

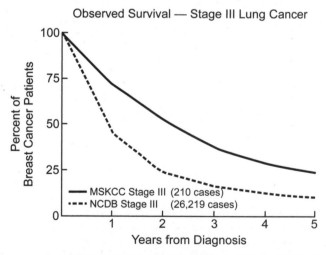

Source: National Cancer Database (NCDB), a collaboration between the American College of Surgeons and the American Cancer Society

Some advanced cancers can be treated effectively, but it can take years to create potent drugs and put them through clinical trials. My development with colleagues of the targeted therapy SAHA, which is used in treating cutaneous T-cell lymphoma, took more than thirty years to develop—which is not unusual for anticancer drugs. Greater use of cancer screening would improve outcomes within just a few years and at much lower cost.

There are two other strategies that can reduce premature deaths even further. Outcomes at top cancer centers like Memorial Sloan-Kettering, which treat the most difficult cancers, are generally better than those at regional hospitals and smaller clinics, sometimes by a wide margin. This is due, in large part, to better diagnostic capabilities and greater experience in treating cancers with the latest drugs and technologies.

For instance, in treating breast cancer, the five-year survival rate for Stage I levels of the disease was 98 percent at Memorial Sloan-Kettering and 95 percent nationally in the 2003–2008 period. At Stage IV, the five-year survival rate was 30 percent at Memorial Sloan-Kettering, compared with 20 percent nationally, according to the National Cancer Data Base. There is a similar divergence of outcomes for other major cancers; Stage I lung cancer patients at Memorial Sloan-Kettering have a 78 percent five-year survival rate, while nationally the rate is about 48 percent.

There are practical factors behind these differences. The advances in genetic and molecular analysis of tumors are making it easier for specialists to develop treatment strategies for each patient that are more likely to hit the right targets and produce better results. This is known as personalized medicine. However, oncologists face a challenge in keeping up with the vast increase in research and information on cancer care. At the major cancer centers, the physicians stay abreast of the research as a matter of course. The challenge is to disseminate the most current information to the thirty thousand or so certified oncologists who practice outside the specialized cancer centers, but who treat an estimated 80 percent of all cancer patients in the United States.

In collaboration with the IBM Watson computer program and the health provider Wellpoint, Memorial Sloan-Kettering is developing a program that will attempt to bring national screening, diagnosis, and treatment standards—and, ultimately, the outcomes—closer to those achieved at Memorial Sloan-Kettering. The Watson computer, which bolstered its reputation by defeating some human champions in the *Jeopardy!* television game show in 2011, is being "trained" to sort treatment data along with enormous volumes of information gleaned from academic journals and other sources. When this computerized database is operating properly, an oncologist will be able to provide a cancer patient's complete diagnosis and record to the system, and it will come back with advice on a treatment program using the most advanced techniques and drugs available. The computer's advice will also reflect the accumulated experience and judgments of top oncologists who have treated similar cases.

The process starts with an accurate diagnosis. There will be an estimated 1.6 million new cases of cancer detected in 2013; roughly 20 percent could be diagnosed incorrectly or incompletely, based on projections by the American Cancer Society. Because a correct early diagnosis is crucial to successful treatment, a poor diagnosis can contribute to higher cancer mortality rates. The new computer program should be able to reduce these errors.

So far, Watson has cross-correlated more than 600,000 diagnostic reports, 1 million pages of medical journal articles, and 1.5 million patient records. On top of that, Memorial Sloan-Kettering's experts in various cancers have tutored Watson in the complexities of diagnosis and treatment. The computer is also absorbing the latest in genetic and molecular research, enabling individually tailored treatments. This program gives physicians across the country access to the best information on almost every cancer. It is online and accessible instantly. Watson is a cloud-based adviser that never forgets.

Watson may also become an important tool for patients, providing clear data on treatment methods, drug side effects, survival rates, and alternative treatments.

seventeen

THE NEXT LEAP

. . . but strong in will
to strive, to seek, to find and not to yield.

—"Ulysses," Alfred, Lord Tennyson

I N 2009 I WAS UNDERGOING a cystoscopy to deal with kidney stones when the doctor spotted something unexpected—cancer in my bladder. Fortunately, the tumor appeared to be small and localized. I had experienced no symptoms, but as a precautionary measure, it was clear to the doctor that it ought to be removed promptly. I was already under general anesthesia, and, as luck would have it, there was an excellent bladder surgeon in the adjoining operating room. I woke to the surprising news that my doctor had found a malignant tumor but that it had been caught early and successfully removed.

About two years later, during a regular follow-up examination, my doctor detected a recurrence of the bladder cancer, which is not uncommon. Back I went to the operating room. This time the surgeon, Bernard Bochner, chief of urology at Memorial Sloan-Kettering, felt that, given the cancer's persistence, I should also have a course of chemotherapy. But I would not be receiving any usual sort of anticancer drug; the standard therapy for my type of bladder cancer is something called Bacille Calmette-Guérin, or BCG, an inactive, genetically engineered bacterium that must be injected directly into the bladder.

I did a little research and was startled to learn that BCG was originally developed in about 1920 as a vaccination against tuberculosis and is still used for that purpose in some parts of the world. Only since 1980 has it found a new use as a bladder cancer treatment.

Why, I asked Dr. Bochner, was this standard TB vaccine effective in stopping only this one type of cancer? He admitted that, aside from speculation on how it may stimulate the immune system to attack cancer cells, medical science had no clear answer. He knew it worked, and that was good enough. Happily, I have remained cancer free since then.

My experience speaks volumes about the state of cancer care. The year 2011 marked the fortieth anniversary of the

National Cancer Act, which launched the "war" on cancer. During the intervening decades, many of the biological mysteries about the ways cancers do their lethal work have been solved. It is one of the great success stories in the history of biology, and perhaps the history of science, involving dozens of remarkable laboratory breakthroughs into the nature of molecular processes. We have learned how cancer cells can at times switch off hardwired genetic instructions controlling when the cells are supposed to die in their natural cycle. We have been developing treatments that reinstate these critical signals so that the cancer cells essentially die a natural death. We understand those mechanisms now in ways we only dimly perceived just three decades ago.

Yet complete knowledge of the biology of cancer is a work in progress, and mysteries persist, such as why a certain bacteria might set in motion a process that kills off bladder cancer cells. It is intriguing and maddening, and it will tax our best scientists and doctors for decades longer. From my perspective, having spent more than sixty years as a leader and as an observer of this race, I believe that we may always find ourselves a step away from a final understanding of the many triggers that transform cells into malignancies and the stratagems the abnormal cells then employ to kill. This is a war that is more about containment than a final victory. I do not think we will ever eliminate the disease so long as cells replicate and we are exposed to the environmental and biological "insults" that can cause genetic abnormalities.

Yet as we succeed in diagnosing cancers earlier and in controlling them, long-term management of the disease is within reach. The real goal is prevention where possible and otherwise early detection of cancers, when the disease is most susceptible to elimination or aggressive treatment. These goals are attainable, something we could not have said just thirty years ago when I came to Memorial Sloan-Kettering.

I decided to write this book in part to describe the extraordinary, if often hidden or poorly understood, leaps scientists have made in understanding the biology of cancer. We began with something close to a blank slate. Cancer has gone from one of the least understood major illnesses to one of the best understood.

I have also undertaken this work to make clear that, although we have found only a few cures—for a small number of cancers—we still face enormous challenges in translating scientific insights into drugs and therapies that extend lives. It may not be the "moon shot" success that President Nixon and Congress envisioned, but we are making a transition from the age of discovery to the age of cancer management, and that is historic.

Our progress has not followed a straight line, and there have been many frustrations. There were blind alleys, new diagnostic tests that produced too many false positives, and drugs that were miraculous in destroying tumors in mice but were disappointing in humans. It is estimated that for every drug that looks promising in animal studies, as few as one in one hundred proceed to clinical trials in humans, and, of those, maybe one in ten can stop the disease effectively.

The heartbreak of this often brutal disease will not just fade away, but a cancer diagnosis is no longer the automatic death sentence it was when, as a young medical student, I had to tell the parents of a smart young teenager that she had an incurable lymphoma. At that time, there was virtually nothing I could do to treat her cancer effectively; today, her disease is nearly always curable in children.

We are moving to an era of "personalized" cancer treatment with therapies customized to fit the genetic signature of a patient's tumor. We begin with an analysis of the DNA of the malignancies of each patient as well as the abnormal cell pathways controlling growth and then tailor treatments to stop those killer cells. Promising new drugs are being developed to impede the overheated metabolism of the cancer cells.

We are working on methods for detecting even one cancer cell within a million blood cells, sort of an ultimate screening test. In time, this blood test for cancer cells will become a routine part of annual health checkups. Such early detection will bring about the next cancer-care revolution.

And the introduction of robotics into cancer surgery holds the promise of further improvements to patient outcomes. With the surgeon operating high-technology machinery from a neighboring room, he need not scrub in for the procedure, saving time and money. The robotic surgeries are producing the same outcomes but with fewer infections and shorter patient stays in the hospital.

These are among the reasons I can say confidently that we are winning the war on cancer. It has been an odyssey, more arduous than many had expected when it was launched more than forty years ago. But the average five-year survival rate for cancer patients has increased by 20 percent in the past two decades. The overall cancer death rate has dropped more than 15 percent since the early 1990s. For certain cancers—such as Stage I or localized breast, prostate, and colon cancer—more than 90 percent are "cured." Many childhood cancers are curable.

The new changes in the paradigms for detection and treatment will accelerate that progress. We will be talking less about lung cancer or liver cancer and more about specific genetic mutations, such as RAS or BRCA1. Anticancer drug research has been enhanced by the identification of these specific genetic and molecular defects, which give the scientists better-defined targets to hit.

Memorial Sloan-Kettering continues to play a significant role in guiding cancer care into this era, now under new leadership, with Craig Thompson as president and Douglas Warner as chairman of the Memorial Sloan-Kettering Cancer Board, Richard Beattie as chairman of the Memorial Hospital Board, and Marie-Josée Kravis as chairman of the Sloan-Kettering Institute Board.

Success in the immediate future may well require tools designed by a room full of marketing experts rather than medical researchers. If more people can be educated and persuaded to get regular cancer screenings—and if President Obama's health care reforms succeed in reducing the costs of preventive measures for low-income families and the newly insured—we know many thousands of lives will be saved or prolonged. There is no rational reason we should tolerate the sometimes large differences in screening rates between the insured and the uninsured or between whites and minority groups. Smart policy can and should overcome the imbalances.

It is heartening to contrast my early, troubling encounter with cancer as a medical student and the responses we now get from patients, such as this one that I received a few years ago from a woman who had been diagnosed with inoperable lung cancer.

Dear Dr. Marks,
Yesterday, after my one year (and 2 months) follow-up testing at the Center my whole team came in grinning, really beaming, and said, congratulations. It all looks great!

And I said, no, the congratulation goes to you guys. And they said, be sure to let Paul Marks know how we did— which I am doing with the greatest of pleasure and once again, without adequate words to thank you.

I ran an institution that had, at the time I left the presidency, a staff of more than seventy-two hundred and a nearly $1 billion annual budget. In 2011 Memorial Sloan-Kettering had twelve thousand staff and a budget of more than $2.5 billion. The new leadership is directing a further $2 billion expansion, including an outpatient surgery center; a leukemia, lymphoma, and bone marrow–transplant day hospital; and a regional facility in Westchester County, New York.

This medical challenge is not just about laboratory successes in unraveling the wiles of our common enemy, but about outcomes, and we now have a historic opportunity to translate the science into improvements through better screening. In this digital age where information is at everyone's fingertips, we can close the gap between the quality of care at the major cancer centers and smaller regional hospitals and clinics. Those achievements will go far toward fulfilling the promise of the scientific leaps we have already taken in the "war" on cancer.

ACKNOWLEDGMENTS

THIS BOOK IS THE STORY OF my long involvement in cancer research and cancer care. It coincides with a remarkable period of progress in understanding in quite intimate detail the biology of the cancer cell and in developing effective approaches to diagnosis, treatment, and prevention of cancers. I have been involved at several levels, including caring for patients; conducting research at the laboratory bench; developing, with colleagues, a new anticancer agent; as chief administrator of the greatest cancer center in the country; and at a policy level as a member of panels and commissions formulating the best approaches to controlling the disease. This book relates how we have reached this point and what we can expect in the future.

I am very grateful to a number of friends who urged me to write this book. In particular Richard "Dick" Beattie, my lawyer, tennis partner, and chairman of the board of Memorial Hospital, deserves my special gratitude. Dick recruited James Sterngold to be my coauthor. Without Jim, you would not have had a chance to read this book. Jim turned my initial manuscript into what I hope is an exciting journey. I am also extremely grateful to Joann Perrone, my marvelous assistant, who participated in the preparation of this book at every step.

My greatest debt is to my wife, Joan Marks, who over the years has taught me so much about life, love, and the pursuit of happiness. She is an icon in her own field—the education of human genetic counselors. She established the first graduate program in this country to train genetic counselors at Sarah Lawrence College. Our three remarkable children, their partners, six grandchildren, and one great-grandchild have added dimensions to our lives that make us proud, grateful, and so frequently very happy.

It is to the many patients for whom we have made a difference that I owe the most—as a doctor and researcher. I got back from their success more than I put into their care and treatment, and that has represented the most rewarding aspect of my career.

Paul A. Marks, MD
New York City
November 2013

INDEX

Index

Index

Index

Index

Index

Index

Index

Obesity, cancer and, 15
Ochoa, Severo, 40
Offit, Kenneth, 158
Oncogenes, 81–82, 95, 194
Oncology, as medical specialty, 7
Opel, John, 159
Oppenheimer, J. Robert, 2
O'Reilly, Richard, 141
Outpatient cancer care, 20, 152–154

p53, 195
Pahlavi, Ashraf, 86
Pahlavi, Mohammad Reza (Shah), 86–87
Pain treatment for cancer patients, 154–155
Palade, George, 43
Pap smears, 203, 205
   access to, 209
   recommendations for, 206
Pasteur, Louis, 29
Pasteur Institute, 29–34, 38, 39, 41
Patient outcomes, improving cancer, 108–109, 135, 217–219
Peer-review panels, 143, 144–145
Penney, Alexandra, 173
Pentose phosphate pathway, 24
Performance reviews, 120

Personalized cancer treatment/personalized medicine, 16–17, 218, 225
Perutz, Max, 42
Pfizer pharmaceutical company, 158–159
Philadelphia chromosome, 58
Philadelphia Inquirer (newspaper), 149
Philanthropic contributions
   Annenberg Haupt, 149–150
   Lauder, 171, 172, 173–174
   Society of Memorial Memorial Sloan-Kettering Cancer Center, 141–142
Pink-ribbon campaign, 173
Polar molecules
   DMSO, 69–76
   effect on leukemia cells, 74–75
   HMBA, 76–78
   toxicity of, 70, 185
Politics of cancer research, 84–85
Pott, Percivall, 201
Presbyterian Hospital, relationship with Columbia University, 46–49
President's Biomedical Research Council, 108
President's Cancer Panel, 20, 68, 94, 208–209

Index

on National Institutes of
  Health, 23
Thompson, Craig, 226
Three-dimensional conformal
  radiation therapy, 197
Three-Mile Island nuclear
  power-plant disaster,
  110–112
Thyroid cancer, 183
Time (magazine), ix, 116
Tobacco, as cause of cancer, 200.
  See also Cigarette smoking
Touch therapy, 163
Transcription, 30–32, 33
Translational research, 162
Transposition of genes, 10
Triangle Publications, 150
Trichstatin A (TSA), 178–179
Trilling, Lionel, 106
TSA. *See* Trichstatin A (TSA)
Tumor cells, genetic analysis
  of, 131
Tyrosine kinase, 58–59, 196

US Public Health Service, 22
University of Chicago
  Comprehensive Cancer
  Center, 91
University of Maryland, 130

Vagelos, Roy, 75–76
Van Doren, Mark, 106

Varmus, Harold, 36, 81–82, 194
Vascular endothelial growth
  factor (VEGF), 195
Virtual colonoscopy, 206, 209
Viruses
  as causative factor in cancer,
  15, 41, 42, 43, 69, 79–82,
  196–197
  retroviruses, 81
Vogelstein, Bert, 195
Vorinostat, 187

Wall Street Journal
  (newspaper), 84
Warner, Douglas, 226–227
War on cancer, 18–19, 60, 61,
  62–64
  emphasis on finding cure,
  x–xi, 12–13, 18, 20, 61
  progress in, 223–228
Watson, James, xii, 11, 21, 40,
  191
Weatherall, David, 138
Weinberger, Caspar, 83
Wellpoint, 218–219
Winawer, Sidney, 205
Women, in medical school,
  51–52

Young, Charles, 122–128
The Youngest Science (Thomas),
  112

251

Paul A. Marks, MD, led the Memorial Sloan-Kettering Cancer Center as president and chief executive officer for nineteen years, beginning in 1980. Prior to his tenure at Memorial Sloan-Kettering, Dr. Marks was professor of human genetics and Frode Jensen Professor of Medicine (1968–1980), dean of the faculty of medicine (1970–1973), and vice president for health sciences and director of the Comprehensive Cancer Center (1973–1980) at Columbia University. Dr. Marks is a member of the National Academy of Sciences and the Institute of Medicine, is a fellow at the American Academy of Arts and Sciences, and has advised the government on science and health research policy. He has published more than 400 scientific articles and received the National Medal of Science from President George H.W. Bush in 1991. Memorial Sloan-Kettering has established the Paul Marks Prize for Cancer Research, given every year to up to three young leaders in cancer research to encourage a new generation of investigators.

CLEMSON SMITH MUÑIZ

James Sterngold is a senior writer for the *Wall Street Journal*, where he reports on finance and business. Jim previously spent eighteen years at the *New York Times*, as a domestic reporter and foreign correspondent in Asia. He shared in a Pulitzer Prize, awarded to the *Times* staff for coverage of 9/11. He has also written for *Fortune, Bloomberg Businessweek, Mother Jones,* and *SmartMoney* magazines and won the Foreign Press Association's award for Best Magazine Financial Article of 2010 and the Magazine Personal Service Award from the Deadline Club in 2012. He is the author of the book *Burning Down the House: How Greed, Deceit, and Bitter Revenge Destroyed E. F. Hutton.*

PublicAffairs is a publishing house founded in 1997. It is a tribute to the standards, values, and flair of three persons who have served as mentors to countless reporters, writers, editors, and book people of all kinds, including me.

I. F. STONE, proprietor of *I. F. Stone's Weekly*, combined a commitment to the First Amendment with entrepreneurial zeal and reporting skill and became one of the great independent journalists in American history. At the age of eighty, Izzy published *The Trial of Socrates*, which was a national bestseller. He wrote the book after he taught himself ancient Greek.

BENJAMIN C. BRADLEE was for nearly thirty years the charismatic editorial leader of *The Washington Post*. It was Ben who gave the *Post* the range and courage to pursue such historic issues as Watergate. He supported his reporters with a tenacity that made them fearless and it is no accident that so many became authors of influential, best-selling books.

ROBERT L. BERNSTEIN, the chief executive of Random House for more than a quarter century, guided one of the nation's premier publishing houses. Bob was personally responsible for many books of political dissent and argument that challenged tyranny around the globe. He is also the founder and longtime chair of Human Rights Watch, one of the most respected human rights organizations in the world.

•   •   •

For fifty years, the banner of Public Affairs Press was carried by its owner Morris B. Schnapper, who published Gandhi, Nasser, Toynbee, Truman, and about 1,500 other authors. In 1983, Schnapper was described by *The Washington Post* as "a redoubtable gadfly." His legacy will endure in the books to come.

Peter Osnos, *Founder and Editor-at-Large*